Marching in Time:

The Colonial Williamsburg Fife and Drum Corps

Marching in Time:

The Colonial Williamsburg Fife and Drum Corps

Phyllis Hall Haislip

ISBN: 0-87517-120-6
Library of Congress Card Number: 2003102137

The Dietz Press
Richmond, Virginia

*For Alex
and the Fife and Drum Corps*

Acknowledgments

The help of many people has made this book possible. I would like to thank the Colonial Williamsburg Foundation for allowing me access to their archives. Special thanks go to the many people associated with the Fifes and Drums who graciously allowed me to interview them. Their contribution is much appreciated.

My most heartfelt thanks to former fifer Alexander Haislip, my son, who patiently answered my many, many questions, sharing with me his insights into the Colonial Williamsburg Fife and Drum Corps. He has read the book to insure accuracy and carefully proofread the manuscript. The book would not have been possible without his support and cooperation.

Charles Jackson and Viky Pedigo contributed photographs. Cathy Grosfils of Visual Resources in the John D. Rockefeller, Jr. Library helped with Colonial Williamsburg photographs. Agnes King continues to provide encouragement, and she contributed a rare background resource. Mary Louise Clifford gave technical advice and support throughout the writing of the book and graciously edited the manuscript. Jim Waldeck validated historical dates and suggested additional material.

Robert Dietz and Wert Smith believed in the project, and with The Dietz Press staff turned photographs and a manuscript into a book.

Table of Contents

Corps members at attention before The Governor's Palace.

The Colonial Williamsburg Fife and Drum Corps

Red uniforms, blue facings, buff knee breeches and vests, tri-cornered hats, shoes with brass buckles. Thirty-six youngsters as bright and shiny as newly minted pennies. The Colonial Williamsburg Senior Fife and Drum Corps poses in front of a photographer.

The Fife and Drum Corps re-creates eighteenth-century military music as part of Colonial Williamsburg's dramatization of daily life in the colonial capital of Virginia. At the time of the American Revolution, all able-bodied men in Williamsburg between the ages of 16 and 60 belonged to the militia. Fifers and drummers were recruited from boys under age 16. More than two centuries after the Revolution ended, it is inspiring to see the Colonial Williamsburg Fife and Drum Corps and remember that young boys once marched off to war.

The Fifes and Drums have just completed a recording of eighteenth-century military music. A photographer on Palace green is taking pictures for the compact disk case and cassette cover. A half-dozen visitors in search of the perfect photograph also snap pictures of the photogenic group. Wherever the Corps goes, whatever they do, they draw an enthusiastic crowd.

Corps members stand stiff and still, the Governor's Palace behind them. The fifers go down on one knee while the drummers arrange themselves in back. Snap, snap, snap. A series of photographs, perfect photographs. But somehow the kids look unnatural . . . lifeless . . . as if waiting for magnesium to ignite and the photographer to emerge from under a dark cloth. A posed photograph can't capture the essence of the Fifes and Drums, nor can a twenty-five-word description.

Something beyond prose and pictures — bigger than mere words and more engaging than panoramic photographs — lies at the heart of the Colonial Williamsburg Fife and Drum Corps. This illusive something is esprit de corps, the sense of camaraderie, enthusiasm, tradition, and commitment to excellence that have characterized the Corps since its inception.

Fifers and drummers practice and play together from age ten until they graduate from high school. They form firm friendships, learn discipline and responsibility, and attain a high degree of musical proficiency. Members believe they are the best at what they do. Numerous awards won by the Fife and Drum Corps since its founding in 1958 attest to its proud tradition of excellence.

The photographer has finished. "Fifes and Drums, DisMISSED!" the sergeant major orders. Like toy soldiers suddenly come to life, the fifers and drummers become energetic kids again, chatting as they hurry off in the direction of the Fifes and Drums Building.

A fifer stoops and picks up a seedpod from one of the catalpa trees that line Palace green. Just as boys must have done in colonial times, he stuffs it in one end of his fife. A flick of his wrist, and the seedpod careens toward another fifer, missing him by inches. The second fifer retrieves the seedpod. He puts it into the end of his fife and a moment later, it lands on the hat of the first fifer. The mock battle continues as the boys disappear up Nicholson Street.

Joining the Corps

It is a gray December afternoon. The fluorescent lights in the Fifes and Drums Building cast a greenish glow over the faces of the recruits who enter the building after school. They socialize as they remove their coats, their quiet talking occasionally punctuated by the slam of a locker door. Backpacks thunk to the floor or are stuffed into cubbyholes or lockers. They take out their music books and get ready for lessons. A few youngsters mill about. Others sprawl on chairs and the gray-green couches. All are waiting for classes to begin. Kaitlyn Woodard, a recruit drummer with a blond ponytail and wire-rimmed glasses, goes to the big drum pad in the main practice room for a few minutes before class. As 4:15 nears, Woodard and the other recruits make their way into the main practice room.

Photograph by David M. Doody, Colonial Williamsburg

A recruit drummer intently studies a music score.

Recruit drummers practice on rubber-topped counter.

The Fife and Drum Corps is known throughout Colonial Williamsburg for punctuality and the recruits realize only a few minutes remain before roll call. Promptly at 4:15, the sergeant major, a Senior Corps member, six-feet tall and formidable to the young recruits, goes to the front of room. "Fall in," he commands. The recruits scurry to find their places. "AttenCHUN," the sergeant major calls out in his deep voice.

Boys and girls scurry into straight lines, facing their senior officer. The littlest boys have the most difficulty coming to attention. Like puppies, their feet seem too big for their bodies. They struggle to stand still, with their hands by their sides, eyes fixed and expressionless.

Drum practice is a serious undertaking for recruits.

Recruits are easy to spot in the Fifes and Drums Building. They are smaller than everyone else and unsure of themselves. It is hard for them to play the right notes on their fifes or time the beats of their drum correctly. They don't yet know how to march and they haven't mastered Corps discipline.

These youngsters, dressed in street clothes, frequently can be seen on Duke of Gloucester Street, carrying their fifes or drumsticks. They eagerly follow the Junior Corps as they march toward Palace green. If the new boys and girls stay in the training program and fulfill the requirements, someday they, too, will wear a colonial costume and perform for visitors.

Recruits are usually ten years old and in fifth grade when the call comes to begin classes at the Fifes and Drums Building on a Saturday morning. Corps Manager, Tim Sutphin, was once a ten-year-old recruit. His wavy hair is graying now, but his appearance is still youthful. He sits easily in his chair at the Fifes and Drums Building as he explains the logic behind the age requirement. "At ten children are starting to gain some independence. Mom and Dad are loosening the ties. It is a perfect time to come into the Corps. Yet there are new rules to follow. There are still parameters to work within."

Each year Colonial Williamsburg recruits about fifteen boys and girls as fifers and drummers. The number varies according to projections of future Corps needs. Joining the Fifes and Drums depends on the applicant's position on a waiting list. Until 1995, it was common for parents, former Corps members, or family friends to sign up a child at birth. Now an applicant has to be at least five years old before he or she can get on the list. Admission into the Fife and Drum Corps is on a first-come, first-served basis. The applicants' parents don't have to work for Colonial Williamsburg, nor do prospective fifers and drummers need any musical ability. They don't even have to live in Williamsburg. They first have to get their name on the list. Then they wait.

Kaitlyn Woodard says, "I like to drum on everything."

In the fall, Corps staff members consult the list. They send applicants who meet the age requirement a letter asking if they are still interested in joining the Corps. From those that respond positively, they compile another list. Then they call prospective fifers and drummers to tell them to report for classes.

On the first day of classes, a family member goes with the recruit to the Fifes and Drums Building. The cost of the initial fife or drumsticks is thirty dollars.

This is the only cost for the eight-year program. The parent brings a copy of the student's most recent report card, establishing that he or she will be able to handle both schoolwork and Fifes and Drums training. This is the last official family involvement with the Corps.

"Some recruits are terrified when their parents leave them," Sutphin explains, speaking with sympathy born from years of Corps leadership. "They are uncomfortable being left in a strange situation. One or two cry. I don't make an issue about it. I tell them to have a drink of water, get themselves squared away, and come back. They are okay when they come back." Woodard recalls, "I wasn't too nervous when my parents left because I knew some of the other recruits."

The Corps uses a peer-teaching system whereby the older fifers and drummers teach the younger ones. This may be something that the recruit has never experienced. And the older kids may be daunting to a recruit. Woodard feels that she is fortunate. One of her drum instructors, Casey Emmett, lives in her neighborhood. Some youngsters who are comfortable taking orders from adults find it difficult to be supervised by other children.

The program has an elaborate ranking system. New boys and girls start at the bottom of the Fifes and Drums hierarchy. Everyone in the Corps, except the other recruits, outranks the newcomers. Even the recruits create their own ranking system based on how many tunes they have passed.

Recruits must master the nuances of the military-style discipline along with learning to play their instruments. From the first day, they stand at attention and respond with a smart, "yes, sir" or "no, ma'am." All business is conducted on a last name basis. The strict discipline of the Corps is often difficult for the new kids. They may have admired the discipline of the Corps during performances, not realizing that the same regimen carried over into the classroom and to other Corps activities. Woodard likes the discipline and thinks that it "has taught me more respect for others." The first few months in the Corps are crucial. "If they stay with it for the first two or two and a half months, they usually stick it out," Sutphin says.

During their recruit year, fifers learn eleven tunes and have to be able to perform them from memory. Drummers must learn 12 tunes and 13 rudiments, the basic patterns that make up drum music. "After you've passed the rudiments," Woodard says, "then it gets hard. You need to get the accents, the beats, and dynamics right, plus the rudiments that you learned."

Once recruits begin the program, they have classes twice a week, and they are required to practice at home. The shrill squeal of the fife is so ear-piercing that Corps members are issued earplugs to use while practicing. Recruits learning the drum may avoid the harsh, high-pitched shock of discordant notes, but they have to get used to the constant drumming of their peers.

How much should the recruits practice? Woodard explains how the staff assigns drum pads to the recruits so they can practice at home. She doesn't limit her practicing to her drum pad, however. "I like to drum on everything," she says, "such as tables, fingers, and even on the side of my chair. Sometimes I drum in school if I have free time." According to the conventional wisdom in the Fifes and Drums Building, a recruit should practice until playing the tune again makes him or her sick. Then, the tune should be played again.

Bill White attests to the enthusiasm of the drummers. White, Executive Producer and Director for Educational Program Development for Colonial Williamsburg, sits in an office overlooking Duke of Gloucester Street. He began his association with Colonial Williamsburg more than thirty years ago as a fifer.

When he hears the Corps on the street, he goes to the square-pained window to watch and remember. He shakes his head and smiles, recalling, "You can still see dents made by over-ardent drummers on the banister of the stairs in Travis House where the Corps was housed from 1965 to 1969." White explains how before the construction of the Fifes and Drums Building, the Corps had a series of homes, one being the small colonial house behind the Market Street Tavern with its permanently scarred banister.

In addition to learning to play an instrument, recruits have drill classes where they practice marching and military discipline. They stand at attention, execute right and

Boys and Girls practice marching in the parking lot.

left wheels, march and countermarch in the parking lot in front of the Fifes and Drums Building or in a nearby horse pasture. "No one likes marching in the horse pasture," former fifer Alex Haislip says.

Woodard finds drill practice both hard and easy. "It is hard," she says, "because you are always at attention and you are not in an air-conditioned room. Also, you have to multitask." She explains how the fifer or drummer has to keep their eyes forward, play their music, keep in step, watch for signals, and maintain the proper spacing. She finds it easy in that "you have other people to back you up. If you miss something, you can listen to what the others are playing and catch up pretty easily." During drill, the sergeant will sometimes whisper the words, "Shucky Ducky," Woodard confesses, "and when he does that, you have to respond 'quack, quack'." If he yells it, the recruits respond in kind. This diversion, taking only a minute or two, is a reminder that these are kids, in spite of the trappings of the military organization. And the exercise in not without its lesson. A recruit must follow orders.

Music and drill are only two aspects of the Fife and Drum Corps. Advancement from recruit to private and all further advancement in the Corps depends on a point system. Recruits earn points for learning tunes, attending classes, and cleaning the study area. They lose points by being late, not knowing their assignment, and missing classes. If recruits lose too many points, they are asked to drop out. The Corps recognizes – on plaques in the hallway of the Fifes and Drums Building – those who earn the most points each month.

A recruit must master an instrument, the nuances of discipline and drill, and the workings of the Corps point system. If all of this isn't daunting enough, the Corps leaders and instructors stress individual responsibility. The boys and girls are responsible for being on time, learning their music, and taking care of their instrument. In addition to these explicit duties, there are implicit expectations. Boys and girls are supposed to be ladies and gentlemen and behave as representatives of Colonial Williamsburg.

Assuming personal responsibility is probably the biggest challenge for a ten year old. For many youngsters, this is their first experience of a world outside of the protection of family and school. Fifes and Drums staff members make it clear that parents are not to meddle in what is the responsibility of Corps members. The recruit's family is used to managing requirements, scheduling, and clothing for other activities, but with the Corps, they must learn to back off.

Sometimes Sutphin has to remind parents, "Your child is in the Corps. You aren't." Yet at the same time he assures parents that he is available if they have questions or want to talk. Woodard likes the fact that her parents aren't involved in the Fife and Drum Corps. "It is really something for the kids," she says.

Not everything associated with the Fifes and Drums is hard work. Before and after classes boys and girls manage to amuse themselves whenever they have a few minutes. A curious boy puts his earplugs into his fife to see what will happen. A drummer clicks her drumsticks together in a Fifes and Drums variation on playing the spoons. Fifes and drumsticks become imaginary dueling swords. And then there are the stories, a whole collection of fifes-and-drums stories that older Corps members pass down to younger Corps members. Woodard says that she hasn't heard many stories, but her instructors are always telling them how hard they had it when they were recruits — the Fifes and Drums version of walking barefoot five miles in the snow to school. Such exchanges become part of the esprit de crops, the cement that holds the group together.

Usually boys and girls spend anywhere from eight to 15 months as recruits. "All you care about is passing tunes," Woodard says, explaining the main thrust of the recruit year. "Sometimes I pass tunes in class. Other times I made an appointment with Mr. Pedigo. The most fun is seeing how far you progress in one short year."

Yet the rigors of the Corps are not for everyone. "If a recruit isn't progressing with his class near the end of the recruit year, he or she may decide to quit or, dig in and work harder," Sutphin says.

Learning new skills takes work. Those who manage to stay the course feel the satisfaction that comes from achievement. Getting a uniform becomes a right of passage, a visible acknowledgment that the young fifer or drummer has mastered the first phase of training.

The day finally comes when the recruit has fulfilled all the requirements to become a private. After passing the last tune and taking a drill test, a staff member tells the recruit to make an appointment at the costume department. Once there, the thrilled fifer or drummer is measured from head to foot. He or she tries on shirts, knee breeches, hats, and shoes. All feel so unlike anything he or she has ever worn, the recruit is unsure whether or not the costume fits. Within a few weeks, the recruit receives a complete colonial costume. Now the youngster is ready to march with the Junior Corps.

Marching with the Junior Corps

Junior Corps boys and girls, dressed in off-white uniforms, emerge from the wooded path near the Capitol and stand around for a few minutes. Their outfits, called hunting frocks or hunting shirts, replicate uniforms worn in Williamsburg by the Second Virginia Regiment during the American Revolution. Every detail of

Photograph by David M. Doody, Colonial Williamsburg

Junior Corps members practice marching in the horse pasture.

their dress, even to their handmade shoes, is historically accurate. Visitors gather, waiting for the performance to begin. The boys and girls stand in groups of three or four, at ease. Just before one o'clock, according to the usual procedure, the drum major, a fifer, and a drummer walk to the center of the street.

The clock on the Capitol strikes the hour. When the clock is silent, the drum major brings the fifer and drummer to attention. The fifer begins to play *Drummer's Call*. After the first phrase, the drummer joins in. These same notes signaled military musicians to gather for duty during the Revolutionary War. The group assembles. The section leader, the highest-ranking fifer in the Junior Corps, yells out the name of the tune, *First of September*. They step off down Duke of Gloucester Street. The visitors, caught up in the moment, follow the Corps.

Attracted by the rattle of the drums and the lilting tune, the moving crowd of spectators grows. Some fall in behind. Others walk abreast of the Corps as it progresses down the street. One old gentleman, ramrod-straight, probably a veteran, marches in step. A dad carries a boy on his shoulders. The boy wears a colonial hat with a great bobbing feather on it. A school group in red T-shirts troops along en masse. Cameras click. Videos roll. Smiles grow.

One rousing tune follows another. The Corps wheels right onto Palace green and marches toward the Palace followed by a swarm of visitors. The drum major signals and the Corps marches in place before coming to a halt. The crowd gathers around as they play *Yankee Doodle* and *Three Taps Three Cheers*. At its conclusion, the appreciative spectators clap, cheer, and some even whistle. "Fifes and drums, disMISSED," commands the drum major. The fifers and drummers break ranks.

Before the children can retreat up Nicholson Street, a plump man with a complicated camera asks a fifer and drummer to pose with his daughter and son. The fifer and drummer are used to being photographed, and they arrange themselves beside a small, red-haired boy and a skinny little girl in pink shorts.

Part of the crowd lingers for a few moments watching the photographer and the Corps members. One photograph leads to another and it is five minutes before the fifer and drummer can join the Corps as they make their way up Nicholson Street.

"The little ones are so cute," a young woman in a wide hat says to her friend. "They can hardly keep up with the others. Their legs are too short."

"Did you see that one in the back carrying a base drum?" her friend replies as they walk away from Palace green. "It's as big as he is."

A big brother takes his little brother's hand. When a family member joins the Corps, the whole family takes interest in the Fifes and Drums, and younger brothers and sisters are likely to follow the tradition.

"The little ones are so cute," a visitor to Colonial Williamsburg says.

Such comments are common after a Junior Corps march. Enthusiastic visitors often speculate on why the littlest fifers and drummers are in the back. And even those who have seen the Corps a number of times may be unaware of the dynamics of the group.

The fifers and drummers are arrayed in the line of march according to rank. The highest-ranking fifers and drummers are in the front lines of their respective groups. Each place in the line of march depends on rank and time in that rank. The fife section leader marches on the front right of the fifers. The drum section leader marches on the front right of the drummers. The corporals assemble in order of rank in the front line with the second highest-ranking fifer or drummer on the far left.

The top-ranking members of the Junior Corps are distinguishable from the other Junior Corps members not only by their place in the line of march. They also have cockades on their hats, carry canteens, and wear leather stocks — the neckpiece worn by military men in colonial times.

This hierarchical arrangement allows the most experienced musicians and marchers to lead the Corps. The newest privates have trouble marching in step and playing at the same time. They haven't learned all the tunes yet. So sometimes they must march along, only pretending to play. On occasion, the smaller youngsters have to struggle to keep up with the pace set by the bigger fifers and drummers. Yet it is these serious little fifers and drummers, trying so hard, who win the hearts of the audience.

A child's first march with the Corps is a big day for the youngster and an occasion for family celebration. Yet it is challenging, too. Lance Pedigo, Corps Supervisor, wears his fair hair long, neatly tied back as was the custom in colonial times. He often can be seen dressed in street clothes in the crowd accompanying the Junior Corps. He began drum lessons at age eight and over three decades has seen many first marches. "There is a lot of awkwardness walking down the street for the first time in a strange costume," he says. "It is not unusual for kids to panic before their first march." On those days, their locker seems particularly difficult to open, and the uniforms unwieldy and hard to get on.

Colonial Williamsburg pays Corps members for performances. The new fifer or drummer will be receiving a paycheck, printed in blue and black ink on a white background. Youngsters are able to earn wages because they have a special status as child performers. They are not paid for the time spent learning their instrument or rehearsals. Their paychecks are often small because actual performance time is only a fraction of the time they commit to Fifes and Drums activities.

Woodard explains excitedly that as soon as she passes all her requirements for the Junior Corps, she will get paid for marches, even if her uniform isn't ready yet. The kids gain real satisfaction from their small paychecks. Former Corps sergeant major Dylan Pritchett, a tall, powerful-looking man, was the Corps' first African-American drum major. He remembers, "My mother is still proud of the fact that she didn't need to buy me shoes or clothes from the age of twelve."

Since fifing and drumming is a year-round, long-term commitment, it is expected that children sometimes will have conflicts between the demands of the Fifes and Drums and their other activities. At these times, the paycheck becomes an incentive to continue with the Corps. "The program at Colonial Williamsburg is unique because the Corps has money," explains Sutphin. "The Corps does not have to depend on volunteers."

Even on cold days the Junior Corps is ready to march.

Volunteers staff most of the fife and drum corps that exist in the United States and around the world. In these units, enthusiasm for the group sometimes has to take a second place to paying jobs. Also, participants must buy their uniforms and equipment. In addition to the kids' small paychecks, the Colonial Williamsburg Foundation provides the Fife and Drum Corps with a special building, equipment, and uniforms.

Once young musicians get used to marching with the Fifes and Drums, their first goal is to move out of the back line of march. They gradually pass tunes and move toward the front. A boy or girl enters the Junior Corps as a private. The next rank is "fifer" for the fifers or "drummer" for the drummers. After passing the requisite tunes, the fifer or drummer eventu-

Junior Corps corporals hone their marching skills.

ally becomes a corporal. Finally, he or she becomes the section leader, the highest-ranking fifer or drummer in the Junior Corps.

Most kids are only thirteen years old when they become section leaders. Visitors see the two most obvious responsibilities of the top fifer and drummer. The highest-ranking fifer in the Corps chooses the tunes and calls them out during performances. The highest-ranking drummer then conveys the command back to the other drummers. The highest-ranking drummer is responsible for selecting drum solos. The same two play *Drummer's Call* before marches.

The authority of the section leaders carries over to activities in the Fifes and Drums Building. Section leaders set the tone for the Junior Corps. The other members look up to them. Sometimes section leaders field problems that are best handled within the group. The roots of leadership start to take hold. Years after his time with the Fifes and Drums, Corps alumnus Michael Sweeney, writes: "Believe it or not, the leadership skills that I utilize as a Naval Officer were first developed as a young fife section leader in the Corps."

Movement into the Senior Corps is regulated by seniority. Section leaders advance into the Senior Corps as openings occur. The greatest number of corporals enter the Senior Corps during the summer following high school graduation. Occasionally, Junior Corps members move up at other times. Vacancies in the Senior Corps may occur when someone moves to another area, drops out, or is asked to leave because of a breach of discipline. Corporals start preparing for the Senior Corps with special classes once a week. In these classes, they begin to learn the Senior Corps repertoire. Finally, the day comes when a staff member tells the fifer or drummer to report to the costume department to be measured for regimentals, the red jackets with blue facing worn by the Senior Corps. The Junior Corps member is ready for promotion.

Junior Corps musicians get lots of experience. They usually perform twice a week during the spring and fall and three days a week in summer. Also, there are special programs where the Junior Corps is featured. Their schedule is especially full during the Christmas season and when the Senior Corps is out of town doing a special show or taking part in a parade.

Even though the Senior Corps is the group most associated with Colonial Williamsburg and the goal of all Junior Corps members, the message to get fitted for regimentals is often greeted with mixed feelings. "Being section leader is big stuff when you're a little kid," Haislip says, "But everybody knows that as soon as you go to the Senior Corps, you'll be back on the bottom."

After having spent two to four years with the Junior Corps, the prospect of learning a whole new repertoire in a couple of weeks can be daunting. Lance Pedigo explains, "The pressure to learn new tunes can be intense."

Junior Corps members may not be in a rush to make the appointment with the costume department. But kids can only drag their feet for so long before they have to face the music. When the new costume is ready, the fifer or drummer must begin the challenges that come with entry into the Senior Corps.

Senior Corps Challenges

The ceremony ends. The Corps exits the Market Square parade field playing *Hey, Johnny Cope* and then signals that *Retreat* is over with the traditional *Three Taps, Three Cheers*. Their march up Duke of Gloucester Street begins with *I'll Towzel Your Kurchy*. A crowd follows. Suddenly, it is apparent that one of the fifers is losing his colonial knee breeches.

Visitors point to the smallest boy in the last row of fifers. "The poor kid," someone murmurs as the Corps marches on, eyes forward.

Stealthily, the boy tries to pull his pants up. His attempt is foiled as the next tune begins. But he never falters.

The fifer's breeches sink lower and lower. He is wearing blue and white boxer shorts. At the end of the block, the breeches are nearly at his knees. Some people point and laugh; the boy's attention never wavers.

Finally, the Corps halts. "DisMISSED," the drum major calls. The boy reaches down and pulls up his pants, thinking perhaps he has recovered his dignity, not realizing that he never lost it. The crowd applauds, and then spontaneously cheers as the fifer calmly walks away with the others.

Fortunately, most new Senior Corps members do not endure the trauma of losing their trousers during a march. Yet moving your possessions into the Senior Corps lockers can be threatening. Everyone in the Senior Corps outranks new corporals. And they have not yet mastered the music and the high standards of performance that characterizes the Senior Corps.

Each member of the Senior Corps occupies a position in rank from one to 36. Seniority based on rank, and the date a member passed into that rank, determines special assignments, participation in Corps governance, and a fifer's or drummer's place in the line of march. Movable tags on the rank board in the main practice room of the Fifes and Drums Building keep track of each member's standing. The competition can be fierce.

Photography by David M. Doody, Colonial Williamsburg

A Senior Corps drummer performs for the photographer.

To achieve the next rank, that of sergeant, a fifer or drummer must pass more tunes, give talks about the history of his instrument, and play solos for an audience. The sergeants are the backbone of the Corps. Only the most dedicated boys and girls strive to qualify for the next step, fife sergeant or drum sergeant, and then for sergeant major, the highest position in the Senior Corps.

There is only one sergeant major at any time. Qualified candidates are considered when a vacancy occurs. Many eligible candidates are disappointed because they have qualified, but an opening doesn't occur.

Author's photographs

Marches begin with Drummer's Call shown in top left photograph. After the fifers and drummers assemble, the section leader in top right photograph is calling the name of the tune for the Corps to play. Bottom photograph shows Tim Sutphin leading the Senior Corps on Duke of Gloucester Street.

Once Corps members earn their rank, they want to keep it. Ambitious younger members push the older ones. Tim Sutphin recalls, "At one point, there were seven or eight qualified sergeant majors. Everyone was afraid the person behind was going to pass him."

Rank conveys status in the Corps, and it also has responsibilities. Senior Corps sergeants teach all the music and drill classes for the recruits, Junior Corps, and Senior Corps. They also act as drum majors for the Junior Corps. "Most of the teachers really care about the well-being of the recruits," Pedigo says. The teachers are both instructors and role models. "I don't think I would have stayed with the Corps if my fife instructor during my recruit year hadn't been Will Bennett," Haislip recalls. "He was patient, supportive, and a darned good teacher."

In addition to teaching, the sergeant major handles the day-to-day functioning of the Corps in the Fifes and Drums Building, and he or she is in charge at performances. "The key to the success of the Corps is giving kids responsibility," observes White. "Kids perform on the street on their own. They handle performances on their own. People are counting on them. Not some boss, but their peers. They learn that they are more effective working as a team than as individuals."

The Senior Corps leadership looks to staff members for guidance. "The Corps is virtually self-directing," Pedigo says. "Staff guide it along, but the highest ranking Senior Corps members assume more and more responsibility." Former Musickmaster John C. Moon explains staff members are caretakers. "They take care that things go as they should," he says.

A lot is going on for the Corps. The Senior Corps presents about 350 programs every year. The Corps performs almost every day from March to December. During the summer, they work as street musicians alone or in groups of two or three. Fifers play penny whistles while drummers accompany them on the bodhran, a small Irish drum. "It's a good way to meet girls," Haislip suggests with a smile.

At special events, fifers and drummers become increasingly conscious of the quality of their performances. "There is a great sense of accomplishment when the Corps performs before thousands of people on the Fourth of July," says Bill White.

Anthony Jackson shows off his regimentals soon after entering the Senior Corps.

Courtesy of Charles Jackson

Haislip recalls the thrill of performing before 12,000 at the Virginia International Arts Festival Tattoo in Norfolk. "We played perfectly for people who really appreciated it," he says. "It was dark when we came out playing. Swoosh, the spotlight hit us. We got a standing ovation. It was like hitting a baseball in the sweet spot."

Occasionally, the fifers or drummers don't meet their high expectations. "The members are miserable when they feel the Corps has performed badly," explains White. Sometimes, blame falls on kids who didn't perform well. Other times, the sergeant major dresses down the entire Corps.

This sense of mutual responsibility creates close bonds among Senior Corps members. These bonds are strengthened during the long hours spent practicing, traveling, and performing. "Not everyone realizes the difference between the Junior Corps and the Senior Corps," says Haislip. "In the Junior Corps you live with your parents. In the Senior Corps, you live with the Corps."

Boys and girls do not, in fact, live with the Senior Corps. It only seems that way because they spend so much time together. In recent years, the Fifes and Drums have fielded a soccer team, and summer evenings find boys who have worked together all week on the playing field. Friendships begun in the Junior Corps are cemented in the Senior Corps and continue into adulthood. Former members often say that their closest friends in high school were other Senior Corps members.

Each year, seniors leave the Corps during the summer after high school graduation. Fifers and drummers traditionally play *Black Bear* during the last march. As part of the tune, drummers yell out the name of the departing member of the Corps.

A graduation ceremony follows the last march. Traditionally, parents weren't allowed at this function. Recently, Corps members wanted family present. "There was family at the first meeting, now family is at the last," Pedigo says.

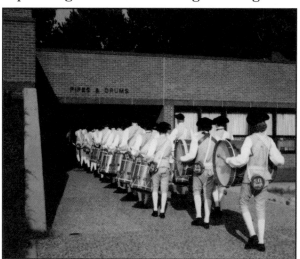

Author's photograph

A graduating senior's last march concludes with the Corps marching into the Fifes and Drums Building where the graduation ceremony will take place.

After the Corps marches into the building, they reform and everyone is put at rest. Staff members review what has happened in the Corps during the time the individual was a member and then add a few personal comments. They officially thank the graduating senior who receives a pewter tankard engraved with his or her initials and dates in the Corps. Corps members come to the front of the room and add any last words of wisdom.

Over the years, Pedigo has seen many graduations. He summarizes typical final comments: "This is the best thing that ever happened to me; The camaraderie is great; The Corps has taught me a lot; Keep the tradition going." It's an emotional moment. Sometimes Corps members let down their guard and cry. Things have come full circle. For some kids their first day with the Corps was an occasion for tears. And now so is their last.

Then the fifer or drummer takes off the familiar uniform for the last time. He or she scratches their name into the paint of their locker, a lasting reminder to new fifers and drummers that they are part of a proud tradition.

More than a Building

It is Saturday at the Fifes and Drums Building. The building stands at the end of tree-lined Franklin Street, half hidden by the earthen berm that surrounds it. The berm keeps sounds inside the building and helps to make it energy efficient. Colonial Williamsburg opened the music building in 1981.

Inside, the main practice hall has special ceiling baffles and perforated, concrete block walls to absorb sound and re-create outdoor acoustics. The room also has two counters with rubber tops for drum practice and mirrors to help drum-

Photograph by David M. Doody, Colonial Williamsburg

"We are as proud of the way we look as we are of the way we sound," says Anthony Jackson.

Courtesy of Charles Jackson

Senior Corps members pose for a casual snapshot in front of the Fifes and Drums Building.

mers play in unison. Another special feature of the building is the drum-storage room. It is vented to maintain the same levels of temperature and humidity as out of doors, preventing drumheads from breaking when taken out of the building. This building is the focal point of the special world of the Colonial Williamsburg Fife and Drum Corps.

This morning, classes are underway throughout the building. Recruit fifers are trying to learn to play *Welcome Here Again.* Their fife instructor, Sergeant Major Anthony Jackson, listens patiently, wondering if this new group will ever learn enough music to make it into the Junior Corps. Jackson is a short, neatly dressed, African-American teenager with an engaging smile. He is universally liked in the Fifes and Drums Building.

One new recruit has been practicing at home. After class he finally feels ready to pass a tune.

"I'd like to try to pass a tune, sir," he says to Jackson.

"All right," Jackson replies. He takes the boy to a practice room. "Do you have your music?"

"Yes, sir," the recruit says.

"Stand and give it a try. Play when you're ready, " Jackson says, closing the door behind them.

The recruit stands uncertainly before he begins playing the first notes of *Chester.* So far, so good. No mistakes. He progresses a bit further, gathering confidence until he plays an *e* instead of an *a*.

Jackson lets the recruit play the tune all the way through. "You've made a mistake," he says when the boy finishes. Jackson takes the music and shows the boy the place where he went wrong. "Try this part over again," he says.

The boy begins again. He is more cautious as he reaches the spot where he had trouble. "Your timing is off." Jackson illustrates the rhythm with a sweep of his hand. "Once more. Put it all together," he says.

The boy is sweating. He takes a deep breath. His initial uneasiness at playing in front of his instructor has passed. He puts the fife to his lips and plays *Chester* perfectly.

"Good," the Jackson says, his voice conveying the real pleasure he takes in the progress of his students. "You've passed the tune!" Jackson notes that in his records and in the proficiency book."

One down for the recruit. Only nine to go.

At the same time, Junior Corps fifers are playing *The White Cockade* together in a sound-baffled practice room while Junior Corps drummers rehearse the same tune in front of the mirrors in the main practice room.

Later that morning, Jackson takes the recruits outdoors for drill practice. The day is bright and warm for November, and kids' faces soon become flushed from the exercise. Orange and yellow leaves swirl from trees as the youngsters march back and forth in the horse pasture that serves as a drill field.

It is almost time to go home when Jackson commands, "Recruits, attenCHUN!" The recruits struggle into place and come to attention.

"If you stand at attention two minutes without moving," he says "you'll get out five minutes early."

Jackson signals three Senior Corps members with a knowing smile. The older Corps members try a series of antics to distract the recruits. An older fifer stands in front of a recruit and sticks out his tongue. There is a smiley-face sticker on it. He crosses his eyes. The recruit doesn't react. A drummer moves into another recruit's space and tickles the recruit's ear with a twig. When this fails, a fifers races up to a recruit from behind. The recruit loses his balance and swerves to one side.

"Too bad," Jackson calls out. "Only three seconds left, and you blew it! Two more minutes, starting now."

The recruits are ready to go home, but they are already learning the strict concentration that will prevent them from being distracted by the visitors to Colonial Williamsburg.

Lessons over, the recruits leave and the Junior Corps members go to their locker rooms to dress for ensemble. All uniforms and other equipment — except for drumsticks, fifes, and socks — are left in the building. Colonial Williamsburg provides washing and cleaning services for uniforms, and each individual is responsible for making sure his or her uniform and equipment will pass inspection. During ensemble the Corps rehearses tunes and formations for the upcoming march.

At one-o'clock the Junior Corps assembles on Duke of Gloucester Street for a march. Corps members get a chance to put into practice what they have learned that morning.

Yet lessons are not over in the Fifes and Drums Building. Jackson teaches Senior Corps classes after lunch. He teaches his peers with the help of the fife section leader. After the section leader takes the roll, the class goes over their assignment. Their assignments are keyed to upcoming performances.

"It's definitely difficult teaching your peers," Jackson recalls telling how the kids he taught in Senior Corps classes were his age and classmates from high school. "It was never stressful though," he says," mostly because everybody almost always knew their stuff. I had a problem one time with three guys who sat along one wall. They were called *The Wall*. They were jokers, and they really irked me. I resolved the problem by calling them to attention. I let them stand there five, sometimes ten minutes. They got the message."

Before every major performance Jackson as sergeant major inspects the Senior Corps to assure highest standards of military-style spit and polish. The inspections themselves only take five minutes, but a lot of careful work precedes them.

During inspection, Jackson approaches each fifer and drummer who snaps to attention with a click of heels. He carefully scrutinizes the uniforms, shoes, and equipment of each fifer and drummer. He penalizes fifers and drummers for not turning out properly. In a system where points count, the penalty hurts. But the desire to maintain high standards for the group motivates the Senior Corps more than the threat of the five-point penalty. "Most of the time everybody takes inspection seriously. Their socks are washed, their shoes are black, their brass shines, and their uniforms are clean, " Jackson explains. "We are as proud as of the way we look as we are of the way we sound."

 Some Senior Corps members stay in the building after classes to practice, chat with each other, sand their leather, and polish brass and shoes. In these odd moments the Corps' oral history is passed on.

Older Corps members recount the collection of anecdotes passed on from former fifers and drummers. Favorites concern catastrophes during marches, such as the story of fifer Dylan Pritchett, who was awarded *The Order of the Black Heart*, when a horsefly bit him so deeply that blood ran down his leg. Of course, he marched on stoically without flinching. There are tales about when the Corps was located in the Up and Down Cottage. All staff offices were upstairs, far from the exuberant antics of rowdy Corps members below. In those days, it is said, the fifers and drummers got away with legendary mischief.

Ever popular stories concern trips. No chewing gum is allowed at programs. At a performance at Langley Air Force Base, the complimentary lunch boxes contained gum. Some young fifers and drummers couldn't resist chewing and were caught. The gum went on their noses, and everyone asked why they had gum on their noses. One story involves a sergeant major who, on the trip to an important performance in Norfolk, Virginia, forgot his pants. He couldn't march and he had to sit and watch the others perform. Such incidents soon achieve legendary status.

If conversation lags, a popular topic is to compare the old Corps to the new. A myth persists that the Corps had a golden age, but no one can agree when, or if, this age existed. The myth of the golden age usually refers to whatever time period the mythmaker was a Corps member. According to Lance Pedigo, "The best Corps is the current Corps." The reason for this, Pedigo believes, is because the Corps is always evolving.

If all else fails, Corps members discuss the relative abilities of fifers and drummers. Each has their own explanation of why recruits have to be ten years old. A fifer explains, "Fifers don't have the necessary lung capacity to play the fife before age ten, while drummers are just too stupid." A drummer counters, "Before age ten drummers aren't big enough to carry the drums, and fifers are just too stupid." These kinds of silly discussions not-withstanding, the Corps and its history are something that all members have in common.

When a staff member isn't in the building, the highest-ranking Senior Corps fifer or drummer is in charge. Sometimes the main practice room becomes the site of an impromptu indoor frisbee or football game. The baffles house a collection of air-born objects from fifes and drumsticks to frisbees and footballs. Jackson recalls playing soccer in the main practice room with a roll of toilet paper stuffed into one of the white, fife-and-drum knee socks. These activities push the limits of permissible behavior. According to Lance Pedigo, "Anything goes, but Corps members know when it goes too far."

Late Saturday afternoon, six Senior Corps members remain in the Fifes and Drums Building. They have an evening presentation at the Conference Center. Since there isn't enough time to go home to eat, they dress and go out together for a quick meal. Staying in character, they visit "The Scotsman's Tavern," a Corps name for a popular fast-food chain with golden arches. Forty-five minutes later, they are back and ready for their program. When their performance is over, they'll return again to the Fifes and Drums Building to change before heading home.

Once a year, usually in January or February, the Annual Corps Meeting is held in the Fifes and Drums Building. It consists of two sessions, one for Corps members and one for parents. The main purpose of the Corps meeting is to discuss the accomplishments of the previous year, review the upcoming schedule, and announce annual awards. This is a time to review what the Corps is doing, describe plans for the future, and make sure members are aware of policy changes and any announcements.

Corps members, in the privacy of their own session, give humorous awards to the staff members, highlighting a foible or recalling an event during the year. A staff member who got the group lost on the way to an out-of-town performance might be given a colossal road map. The fifers and drummers receive numerous other awards, most focusing on the biggest faux pas of the previous year. A fifer who drank too many sodas and got sick

Author's photograph

Every year, Viky Pedigo, the mother of Corps Supervisor, Lance Pedigo, provides a Christmas tree for the Fifes and Drums Building. The tree decorations are fifes and drums except for the tricornered hat at its top.

on a trip might receive Rolaids or a drummer whose pants fell down might be given a rope to hold them up.

During the parents' session, the top members of the Senior Corps march into the meeting room. They usually choose the most challenging part of their repertoire, showing off their considerable skills to an appreciative audience. A reception follows.

Parents take this opportunity to look around the Fifes and Drums Building.

Plaques, inscribed with the names of outstanding fifers and drummers, line the main lobby walls. Cases display trophies won by the Corps over the years in various fifing and drumming competitions. Here, too, is a soccer trophy from the year the Fifes and Drums won their division championship.

In describing the importance of the Corps in the lives of its members, Lance Pedigo explains that the thing that makes it so special is that youngsters "grow up with it, passing through all the stages of adolescence as a Corps member. The Corps is a long-term commitment separate from the world of both parents and school." The center of this separate world is the Fifes and Drums Building.

Great Performances

Visitors to Colonial Williamsburg may see a number of different performances of the Fifes and Drums. In fact, many return to the colonial capital frequently because the programs are continually changing, offering new insights into life in Williamsburg in the eighteenth century. From very specific programs like the reenactment of the Burning of Lord North in effigy to regular, twice-weekly marches, the Corps can frequently be seen on Duke of Gloucester Street. One of the highlights of the year for the Corps, and for visitors, is the Fourth of July.

Courtesy of Colonial Williamsburg

During a pre-revolution protest reenactment of the burning of Lord North in effigy, the Senior Corps escorts the militia.

Excitement begins to grow in town about dinnertime. People arrive early. Parking places all over town disappear. Ingenious drivers commandeer vacant lots, school playing fields, and private College of Williams and Mary parking spaces. All usual parking places are filled. Some enthusiasts drive over a sidewalk and park in a deserted field. Everyone walks toward Duke of Gloucester Street and the center of the restored town.

All over town people carry lawn chairs, blankets, and umbrellas. They push wheelchairs and baby strollers. Some people wear red, white, and blue. Others wave flags. A few have sparklers or novelty, light-up hats. They search for an ideal place to see the Fifes and Drums and the fireworks. By dusk it is almost impossible to make your way along Duke of Gloucester Street.

Special areas have been designated and roped off for the Senior Corps to march on Palace green and for the Junior Corps to perform in front of the Powder Magazine. Crowds ring the roped-off areas. People talk and children chase each other as darkness descends. When the music starts, the crowd grows quiet and presses eagerly forward, hoping to glimpse the performers. Visitors and locals stand eight deep, trying to see the Fifes and Drums.

The Fifes and Drums march in the confined spaces. Back and forth, executing countermarch after countermarch in order to change direction in the limited space. They play two-hundred-year-old songs, jaunty and jubilant

The Senior Corps performs at Montpellier, home of President James Madison.

pieces celebrating our nation's heritage. They perform for 45 minutes before an enthusiastic audience. When the Corps finishes, it is completely dark. Time for the fireworks to begin.

July Fourth, American Independence, Colonial Williamsburg, fireworks, the Fifes and Drums. Everyone is in a festive mood. Somehow it all fits.

Boom! A bright cluster lights the sky, followed by another, and yet another. More booms follow. Many-colored starbursts, giant mushrooms, light the sky. It wouldn't be the Fourth of July without fireworks, and at Colonial Williamsburg they are spectacular. As the program draws to a close, three giant fountains of sparks begin to rise from the ground and spew forth light. A murmur of delight ripples through the crowd. Boom, flash, crash, fireworks explode in a grand finale. Everyone claps and cheers.

The Senior Corps leaves Palace green, marching and playing. They head toward the Courthouse where the Junior Corps has been watching the fireworks. Meanwhile, the Junior Corps forms up, standing at attention, on Duke of Gloucester Street in front of the Powder Magazine. The Senior Corps approaches. To the amazed delight of the crowd, the Senior Corps marches through the Junior Corps ranks. Once the Senior Corps is in front, both march off together, playing *Chester*. Spectators follow the Fifes and Drums as they progress along darkened streets toward the Capitol. Performances and fireworks have given way to a parade.

Many people follow the Fifes and Drums, accompanying them from the center of town up Duke of Gloucester Street to Botetourt Street and Nicholson Street. The Senior Corps and Junior Corps play tunes alternately. As they near the path leading to the Fifes and Drums Building, some spectators stop, assuming this will be the end of the march. At a signal from the drum major, Corps members turn and march off by twos along the path and through the parking lot, playing as they go. The crowd follows.

Courtesy of Fifes and Drums Archives

During the annual Tattoo at USAF Air Combat Command, Langley Air Force Base, Virginia, the Senior Corps marches past modern day aircraft.

Author's photograph

Senior Corps members entertaining visitors arriving at the Colonial Williamsburg President's house for a Christmas party.

The youngsters march into the Fifes and Drums Building still playing. The sound of the music becomes muffled. Part of the crowd enters the building along with the musicians. It is as if these enthusiastic followers don't want the evening to be over. They don't want the Fourth of July to be over. They don't want the fifers and drummers to become ordinary kids, dressed in jeans, T-shirts, and too big shoes.

Fourth of July is one of two days each year that both the Senior and Junior Corps perform at the same time. The other occasion is Grand Illumination when Colonial Williamsburg begins the Christmas season with the lighting of the city and a spectacular display of fireworks.

Throughout the holiday season, almost every evening some area of the Historic District is illuminated. During these performances, the Fifes and Drums provide music to accompany the official lighting of notable houses and other buildings. Bonfires and braziers filled with blazing wood chips cast shadows on the dark streets. Fifers and drummers march along, accompanied by men carrying flaming torches. The darkness and drama carry spectators back to a simpler time.

The *Tattoo*, sometimes performed during the Christmas season, is a great favorite. Tonight, it is cold and dark. On Duke of Gloucester Street, flames leap into the darkness from four great bonfires. Visitors cluster around the fires drawn by the warmth and the cheerful crackling of logs.

The Fife and Drum Corps stands at ease in a darkened side street, not yet ready to march. The wind blows. Sparks shower three or four spectators who back away from the fire.

Finally, the narrator explains the purpose of this evening's ceremony. In colonial times, *Tattoo* may have referred to the drum beat, tap-too or it may have been a corruption of the words "taps to" meaning it was time to close the taverns. It was a signal for the innkeepers and sutlers to shut the taps on their beer casks and close shop for the day. *Tattoo* was usually held at 9:30 p.m. although General Washington in one directive stipulated eight o'clock in winter and ten o'clock in summer.

The explanation over, the ceremony begins with *Drummer's Call*. The fifers and drummers assemble in the street. The provost detachment of the colonial militia falls in behind the Corps. It will be their task to roust the soldiers out of the taverns. Militiamen with lighted torches stand at the four corners of the Corps. With the click of their heels hitting the pavement in unison, the Corps comes to attention. A moment later, they begin to play *Devil's Dream*. The whole group sets off toward the Capitol.

They come first to Wetherburn's Tavern and stop. The fifers and drummers entertain the crowd while the provost's men scurry into the tavern. Members of the militia are supposed to leave the taverns and fall in behind the Corps, but some of the militia are in their cups and unwilling to end the night's revelries.

A few moments later the provost's detachment returns with rowdy militiamen who with burps, hiccups, and protests fall in behind the Corps. The crowd laughs and claps enthusiastically at the antics of the colonial performers. The drum major commands: "Forward, march." And the group is off down the street.

The Corps halts at each tavern, playing more tunes while the provost's men round up more militiamen. At Raleigh Tavern everybody must be having an especially good time. One soldier comes out wearing a woman's bonnet. Another tries to bring along his female friend to the delight of the spectators.

Near the Capitol, the Fife and Drum Corps, followed by a collection of befuddled militiamen, comes to a halt. The provost marches off with the unruly soldiers. They will return to camp for a final roll call. The Fifes and Drums Corps plays a final tune, followed by *Three Taps, Three Cheers* to signal the ceremony is over. The drum major dismisses the Corps, and they quickly disperse.

The visitors who had followed the Corps to the Capitol turn back toward Market Square. It is still dark and cold. The wind that had showered sparks earlier from the bonfires has picked up and the temperature has dropped. Yet the mood has lightened. Certainly, this is a favorite Christmastime performance, linking modern Americans to their colonial predecessors through humor and music.

Origin of Fifing and Drumming

The Colonial Williamsburg Fife and Drum Corps is part of a tradition that stretches back more than five hundred years. Curiously, no comprehensive histories of fifing and drumming exist. Nonetheless, fifers and drummers appear in many books, documents, and memoirs.

The fife and the drum may have originally come into Europe from Turkey. The Swiss first used the fife in military operations, probably at the end of the fifteenth century. Before the advent of national armies, the Swiss were the foremost mercenaries in Europe. Their rise to prominence is associated with changes in warfare brought by the displacement of the medieval knight by massed infantry. To coordinate the infantry armed with pikes — spears with pointed ends— and later with muskets, the Swiss used fifes and drums to communicate on the battlefield. The fife could be heard above the rattle of musket fire and the drum below the roar of the cannon.

Since the Swiss were mercenaries and found employment throughout Europe, it is not surprising that fifing and drumming soon spread to other countries. Historical records mention fifes and drums in Germany in 1511. In France an *Ordonnance* of King Francis I from 1534 called for two fifes and two drums for each 1000 soldiers. The French writer Rabelais mentions "merry fifes and drums" in *Gargantua and Pantagruel* published in 1535. King Henry VIII of England sent to Vienna to obtain fifes. Records of a muster of Londoners in 1540 mentions "droumes" and "ffyffers." Shakespeare mentions fifing and drumming in two plays. In *Othello*, he refers to "the ear-piercing fife," and to the "vile squealing of the wry-necked fife" in *The Merchant of Venice*. English state papers reveal complaints from commanding officers about the scarcity of musicians. Apparently, fifers and drummers would only sign up for a month at a time, demanded high wages, and were undependable. They were described as "easy players" and "very drunkards."

Part of the problem in obtaining fifers and drummers in the sixteenth century was that they had extensive duties. Englishman Ralph Smith in 1553 wrote about their importance in negotiations. They should be "faithful, secret and ingenious." They should know languages because they would often be "sent to parley with enemies" and "redeem and conduct prisoners." Apparently, fifers and drummers were used extensively as envoys to foreign powers on field negotiations in battle. Smith also lists additional duties, they must practice "their instruments, teach the company the sound of the march, alarm, approach, assault, battle, retreat, skirmish, or any other calling that of necessity would be known." The fifers and drummers usually wore gaudy clothing into battle to proclaim their status as non-combatants.

What it might have been like to be military fifers or drummers during these early years has largely been lost. The *Autobiography of Benvenuto Cellini* provides a window into the status of Italian musicians working for the government of Florence. Cellini was a sixteenth-century Florentine goldsmith and sculptor. His father played the fife for the government of Florence first "merely to amuse himself ... then they pestered him into becoming a member of their band ....." The autobiographer takes pains to explain, "In those days the musicians were all members of the most respected trades, and some of them belonged to the greater guilds of silk and wool." Although the elder Cellini wanted his son to follow in his footsteps as a musician, the future artist "was never more miserable" than when his father talked to him about it. Cellini's father eventually relented and let his son become a goldsmith. A friend urged the elder Cellini: "Your Benvenuto will get much more honor and profit if he studies how to be a goldsmith than he will out of all this fifing nonsense."

Armies and cities employed fifers and drummers throughout the fifteenth and sixteenth centuries, but it was in the seventeenth and eighteenth centuries that the military musicians became essential. As national states began to emerge and national armies developed to support the states, the use of fifes and drums grew more widespread. Armies changed from the Swiss model, described by historian Michael Roberts in *The Military Revolution* as "a brute mass" to "an articulated organism of which each part responded to impulses from above." Standing armies replaced undependable mercenaries. Soldiers began to march in step and wear uniforms, two important indications of the subordination of the individual to the group. As the armies grew in size and sophistication, they required effective administrative support in order to pay the soldiers, provide uniforms, training, and equipment. The fifes and drums became a fundamental part of the drill and discipline that made the national armies effective military units.

These new national armies required new tactics and strategy. John Moon, former Musickmaster at Colonial Williamsburg, writes that the advanced block

Fifers and drummers accompany the General Edward Braddock on the march to Fort Duquesne in 1755 during the French and Indians Wars.

and linear formations "required soldiers to drill, maneuver, and fight in teams rather than on an individual basis." In addition to utilizing fifes and drums for communication, there had to be "regulations that governed marching in step, warning signals, and musical calls for various functions to be performed at definite times." Regulating the length and tempo of the steps enabled troop commanders to prepare time and movement tables.

The Colony of Virginia as far back as 1633 employed drummers for militia practice. By 1687, Virginia purchased musical instruments for the militia. The Dutch in New York provided drums for their militia. At the time of the French and Indian Wars (1689-1763), fifers and drummers were field musicians for British, French, and American troops.

At the end of the seventeenth century and throughout the eighteenth century, soldiers performed an elaborate ballet on and off the battlefield. The fifes and drums orchestrated this ballet. The eighteenth-century soldiers, in impeccable uniforms, marching in perfect order, became the model for legions of toy soldiers enjoyed by generations of children.

The American Revolution

From the distance of the twenty-first century, it is hard to comprehend the role of fifes and drums in the War of Independence. They were the timekeepers of the army, regulating the soldier's day from sun up to sun down. The Continental Army could not have run efficiently without the calls and ceremonies of the fifes and drums. In addition to their daily duties, fifers and drummers performed for celebrations, parades, and entertainments. Their most important role, however, was on the battlefield. In an age of telecommunications, the limitations of the human voice can easily be overlooked. But at the time of the American Revolution, the fife and drum corps was the voice of the generals. Without them, the commanders would have no way to make their orders known.

Fifers and drummers were present at Lexington and Concord, the first battles of the Revolutionary War. After a one-sided victory at Lexington, the British headed to Concord to destroy the militia's supplies on April 19, 1775. The Americans, advancing with fifes and drums playing, attacked the British at the North Bridge. Three weeks later, fifers and drummers played for a celebration after Ethan Allen and his Green Mountain Boys took Fort Ticonderoga from the British on May 10, 1775.

Reading the Declaration of Independence before Washington's Army in New York city, July 9, 1776.

Drawing by Howard Pyle, Harper's Monthly, July 1892.

In the days that followed these early clashes, the colonists began recruiting an army. An advertisement appeared in the *Virginia Gazette* in 1775. Thomas Sterling and Thomas Hookins stated that they would be "willing to learn any number of boys the Military Musick of the Fife and Drum for a fee." Later that year, advertisements appeared for drummers and fifers "who can teach others the Duty, to act as Drum and Fife Majors."

Congress established the Continental Army on June 14, 1775. In the American army each company, containing between sixty and one hundred men, had a fifer and drummer. Eight companies composed a battalion and two battalions made

Baron von Steuben at Valley Forge established a manual of military practices for the Continental Army.

up a regiment. A regiment, then, would have at least sixteen fifers and sixteen drummers. The massed fifers and drummers became the "field music" of the regiment.

Fifes and drums played a role in recruiting the new army. Stirring music helped to promote the colonial cause. Many young men got caught up in the excitement and wanted to join a regiment. A man named Philip Fithian describes the situation in Virginia where drum beats summoned the inhabitants at five each morning: "Mars, the great God of Battle, is now honored in every part of this spacious Colony, but here every Presence is warlike, every sound is martial! Drums beating, Fifes and Bag-Pipes playing and only sonorous and heroic Tunes — Every man has a hunting shirt which is the Uniform of each company."

Once an army was recruited in Virginia, General Andrew Lewis, the commander of the troops at Williamsburg, appointed a fife major and a drum major in 1776. Their job was to teach fifers and drummers incidental music for ceremonies and the duty calls and signals necessary for the regiment. Lewis required the young fifers and drummers, most of whom entered the military without musical training, to practice each day between eleven and one o'clock. It was usual for the fifers and drummers to practice two hours a day. However, one colonel increased that to four, a fact that speaks to the lack of musical ability of the fifers and drummers, and the real necessity that they should function proficiently.

The morals of the young fifers and drummers were in the care of their commanding officers. Parents of 1776 would have been reassured to see Andrew Lewis'

Orderly Book. He instructs the officers of the companies in the 6th Virginia Battalion "to train the youths under their particular care" in morality as well as in military matters. In spite of Lewis' directive, it still must have been difficult when war came to see a beardless boy of ten or 12 go marching off to an uncertain fate with grown men.

In Virginia, a young fifer or drummer could serve with a regular army unit or with the local militia. If he joined the militia, he would be part of a citizen army since every man between 16 and 60 had the obligation to serve in the militia. And the militia contained the stalwart citizens, the rowdy youths, the backwoodsmen, and every shade of class and character in the society. As such, it was much different from the professional British Army. Fathers, brothers, neighbors, and friends could all be part of the same company. And there were other youngsters in the militia. If a young boy marched off into manhood with the Virginia militia, he didn't necessarily go alone.

Fifers and drummers in both the militia and the regular army played the music that organized military life in camp or garrison. From sunrise to lights out, they ordered the Continental soldiers' day. The earliest assembly of the soldiers was with *Reveille* at sunrise. The commanding officer inspected the troops and gave the orders of the day at *Assembly*. The soldiers quit work at sunset when they attended the *Retreat* ceremony. There was no *Taps* in the Continental Army to signal "lights out." Instead soldiers returned to their tents at *Tattoo* where they were to remain until *Reveille* the next morning.

In the early days of the war, the colonists modeled the Continental Army on the British Army, adopting Harvey's *Manual of Arms, King's Regulation* published in 1764. As the war progressed, General Washington saw the need to standardize military practices. He asked Baron von Steuben to write a manual of military practices. Von Steuben's *Regulations for the Order and Discipline of the Troops of the United States* went into effect on March 29, 1779. These regulations remained in effect without change until 1824. In this manual, Von Steuben prohibited voice commands and outlined the calls necessary for the fifers and drummers: *The General* — strike tents and prepare to march, *The March*, *The Troop* — daily trooping of regimental colors, *To Arms*, and *The Parley* — when a conference with the enemy is desired.

Along with the calls, von Steuben listed twelve signals that the fifers and drummers had to know and the troops had to recognize. Typical signals might be to go for wood, assemble for a fatigue party, or prepare for church. The fifers and drummers had to learn all the calls and signals for the Continental Army and teach them to the army. The soldiers had to be sufficiently familiar with the calls so that they could easily distinguish one from another, a crucial skill in battle. Marching to the beat of a different drum could be fatal in wartime.

Fifers' and drummers' duties were not limited to the prescribed ceremonies, calls, and signals. When dignitaries, such as foreign ambassadors, visited the Continental Army, the fifes and drums saluted them. They also furnished the music for parades. On one occasion, General Washington marched through Philadelphia, arraying his troops eight across. The company musicians — 80 to 120 fifers and drummers — formed the center of each brigade.

Whenever there was a celebration, the fifes and drums performed. In October, 1777, after the Continental Army under General Gates defeated the British under General Burgoyne at the all-important Battle of Saratoga, the fifes and drums played *Yankee Doodle* during the surrender ceremony. At a May Day gathering after Valley Forge, the soldiers paraded around a maypole to the music of the fifes and drums.

On a more somber note, fifers and drummers had the solemn duty of playing at military funerals. Then the drums were shrouded and muffled. Often they played *Roslin Castle* or *Dead March*.

Fifers and drummers had other unpleasant duties. They officiated when a soldier convicted of a crime or a breech of discipline was drummed out of camp. Typical crimes might be stealing, assault, or desertion. At the siege of Boston men were drummed out of the army for drinking to British General Gage's health and cursing the American army. Typically, the musicians paraded the prisoner before the regiment to the tune of *Rogues March*. They escorted him to the entrance of the camp. There, his coat was turned inside out and his hands tied behind him. A kick from the youngest drummer sent him on his way. The fifers and drummers might also play *Rogues March* if a soldier married the widow of a fallen comrade. Fifers and drummers performed when someone was sentenced to corporal punishment. For this purpose some drummers carried the cat-o-nine-tails in a red-flannel bag.

Often when they had a few leisure moments in camp, the soldiers called upon them for entertainment. They played an important role in bolstering the sagging morale of the rag-tag Continental Army. Many a weary hour was eased with a few merry tunes from the fifers and drummers. They played marches, dances, gavottes, jigs, allemandes, hornpipes, and reels. Their repertoire included tunes by eigh-

An engraving by J. Rogers of a Thrumbull painting in: Benson John Lossing, *Washington and the American Republic*, Vol II (New York: Virtue & Yorston, c1870), p.338.

A wounded drummer at the Battle of Princeton where General Washington defeated the British on January 3, 1777.

teenth-century composers such as Handel, Hayden, Mouret, Telemann, Mozart, and Beethoven.

The most significant role of fifers and drummers was on the battlefield. Their contribution to the success of the battle is not always mentioned because they were not separate from the army, but an integral part of it. In one instance, at the Battle of Bennington on August 16, 1777, the fifes and drums incited the American attack. Colonel John Stark's fifers and drummers advanced directly at the enemy, giving the soldiers the inspiration they needed to defeat the British. The young fifers and drummers playing patriotic tunes or forwarding the generals' commands must have inspired many soldiers throughout the war.

Fifers and drummers had a high profile in the Continental Army because of their involvement in so many aspects of military life. This did not mean, however, that they were always praised. General Washington wrote that the music of the Army was "in general very bad" and he expected "that the drum and fife Majors exert themselves to improve it, or they will be reduced, and their extraordinary pay taken from them." He mandated that hours for practice be assigned and concluded. "Nothing is more agreeable, and ornamental, than good music; every officer, for the credit of his corps, should take care to provide it." Under

Washington's reforms, a musician couldn't perform with a regiment until he had the approval and recommendation of his fife or drum major.

It was possibly Washington's dissatisfaction with the music of fifes and drums that led to the appointment of an Inspector and Superintendent of Music for the Army. Lieutenant John Hiwell had been at Valley Forge with Baron von Steuben and was familiar with the new regulations. Hiwell's job was to supervise all the fife and drum majors in the Continental Army. He requisitioned supplies, enforced disciplinary standards, established performance standards, and inspected musical instruments.

Beside the significant role they played in military life, an inducement for a boy to join the fifers or drummers was that musicians received better pay than regular soldiers. When Congress on May 27, 1778, voted a reorganization of the army, fifers and drummers got the same pay as a corporal, that being $8.33 per month. This was 60 cents more than a private received. A young fifer or a drummer in the artillery was paid $8.67 a month. If a father joined the army as a private and the son joined the fifes and drums, the son would get higher pay than his father. This pay disparity, however, might not have mattered very much since the Continental soldiers were infrequently paid. Joseph Martin, in his memoir, *Private Yankee Doodle*, reports being paid for service in 1776, and for one month in 1781 and "except for that, I never received any pay worth the name while I belonged to the army." Martin served from 1776 to the war's end in 1783.

Better pay was one motivation for joining the fifes and drums. Another was the light work. Boys as young as nine or ten could become fifers and drummers because musicians did not have to engage in heavy labor such as trench building.

Fifers and drummers were non-combatants. If young men wanted to go off to war and had the obligation to join the militia at age 16, perhaps it was just as well that a boy entered military service as a non-combatant with better pay.

Being a non-combatant meant more than it does in the twenty-first century. Modern weaponry for all its sophistication often cannot distinguish combatants from non-combatants. The eighteenth-century armies waged war according to certain rules, and one of the rules protected non-combatants. Fifers and drummers signaled their non-combatant status by wearing uniforms, reversing the colors of their regiment. In the case of the State Garrison Regiment with headquarters in Williamsburg, Virginia, the uniform was blue with red collars and cuffs called facings. The fifers and drummers had red uniforms with blue collars and cuffs. These reverse colors were also on the regimental drums.

This Philadelphia engraving from 1780 shows fifers and drummers accompanying a procession on the way to burn an effigy of the traitor Benedict Arnold.

A common depiction of armies in the eighteenth century shows two opposing ranks marching up to each other and firing point blank. The Continental Army fought that way in the Revolutionary War, but they also fought in non-traditional ways. In his General Order of October 27, 1776, General Washington urged his men to fight from the cover of woods and stonewalls. It may be that non-traditional warfare changed the status of the fifes and drums. It may also have been that young musicians grew into mature men.

An entry in the *Journals of the Continental Congress* from August 23, 1777, specifies that "all able bodied fifers and drummers be obliged to do duty as soldiers and be furnished with arms." As the war dragged on, some of the fifers and drummers were no longer young boys, and yet they still refused to do guard, sentry, police, or other duties. This congressional order could not be enforced since it violated the musicians' terms of enlistment. However, the directive that they should be furnished with arms seems to have been carried out. When the war was over, official records reveal that fifers and drummers were allowed to take home their instruments, but not their guns.

Congressional concern with the problem of older fifers and drummers did not disappear. A later entry in the *Journals of the Continental Congress* for December 24, 1781, reads: "Nothing is more common than to see men employed in the duty [fifing and drumming] who are in every respect fit for soldiers, whilst boys hardly able to bear arms are put into the ranks ...." Congress resolved that no recruits would be enlisted as fifers and drummers, and that when needed, fifers and drummers "shall be taken from the soldiers of the corps." If fifers and drummers were recruited from the corps, there would then be no special terms of enlistment to prevent the fifers and drummers from performing the duties of soldiers.

Information is scarce about individual fifers and drummers who served in the Revolutionary War. One intriguing Revolutionary War pension record is that of Hamet Achmet, an African American who had once been a servant of General Washington. Susan Cifaldi, assistant archivist of The Company of Fifers and Drummers has published his story. The young man ran away to Middletown, Connecticut, where he enlisted in the First Connecticut Regiment as a drummer. He fought at Stony Point, was wounded at Germantown, spent the winter at Valley Forge, and was at the Battle of Yorktown. In the 1840 Census of Revolutionary War Pensioners he is listed as being 81 years old.

Black Americans fought in the Continental Army and the British Army during the Revolutionary War. Runaway slaves usually joined the British or their German allies who offered them freedom in return for military service. Since many of the escaped slaves were very young, they often became fifers and drummers. Hessian records reveal 83 black drummers and 3 black fifers during the years from 1777 to 1783.

A land grant bounty application reveals another tantalizing story. Fife Major William Holliday was a member of the State Garrison Regiment stationed in Williamsburg. He resigned from the regiment in May 1779 and enlisted on the brig *Fanny.* A British privateer captured the vessel and took Holliday prisoner. He spent five months aboard a prison ship in New York Harbor before being exchanged. On the return trip to Virginia, he was shipwrecked and spent ten years in the West Indies. On his return to Virginia in 1791, he applied for a land grant bounty.

The experiences of Achmet and Holliday were unusual. The day-to-day lives of fifers and drummers did not make it into the records. Yet there must have been many a tale, told years later of the adventures of the young men who went to war in the great experiment of the American Revolution.

The Virginia State Garrison Regiment

The Colonial Williamsburg Senior Corps recreates the field music, the collected musicians, of the Virginia State Garrison Regiment. In May of 1778, the Virginia General Assembly authorized the establishment of a regiment for the protection of Virginia. The regiment was to be a unit of the regular army, not the militia. Regiments, raised earlier in the war, were on duty outside of Virginia with the Continental Army, and a force was necessary to defend Williamsburg, protect the Powder Magazine, and man the fortifications in York, Hampton, and Portsmouth.

The new regiment, commanded by a colonel, with a staff of a lieutenant colonel and a major, was to have eight companies and at full strength had 544 men. The governor and his council gave commissions to officers when they had raised their quota of troops. A captain, two lieutenants, an ensign, and four sergeants headed each company.

The field music of the new regiment consisted of around 20 fifers and drummers. Each company had one fifer and one drummer, and the commanding officer and his adjutant both had a fifer and a drummer in their service. A fife major and a drum major probably headed the group of musicians.

The State Garrison Regiment received the same pay, rations, and bounty as the soldiers in the Continental Army. At this time, the pay for the rank and file was $8.67 per month plus rations. Their clothing allotment included two shirts. They were probably hunting shirts, made of coarse linen material coming to their knees and almost covering their breeches. By April of 1779 the State Garrison Regiment had blue regimentals with red facings.

On August 14, 1779, the Governor of Virginia, Thomas Jefferson, commissioned Charles R. Porterfield as a Lieutenant Colonel in the State Garrison Regiment. Porterfield was from Frederick County, Virginia. At the age of 25, he had joined Daniel Morgan's Company and he had fought under General Benedict Arnold at Quebec. According to John Marshall who later became Chief Justice of the United States, Porterfield was the first person to cross the barricade when Arnold stormed the heights at Quebec on December 31, 1775. Porterfield along with Morgan and most of the attackers were captured at Quebec where they remained until late in 1776. The *Virginia Historical Magazine* has published excerpts of Porterfield's diary from his imprisonment at Quebec. In October of 1777, Porterfield fought at the Battle of Saratoga. He spent the winter of 1777-1778 at Valley Forge where John Marshall was one of his messmates.

The War of Independence was going badly for the Americans in 1779 when Jefferson gave Porterfield his commission with the State Garrison Regiment. The British under General Cornwallis, the leading general of his day, had turned their attention to capturing the south. The Continental Congress sent Virginia troops to the relief of Charleston, under siege by Cornwallis.

The soldiers of the State Garrison Regiment under the terms of their enlistment were not to leave the state. Yet more men were needed for the relief of Charleston. Porterfield raised a special light infantry unit of volunteers at his own expense. Light infantry units, composed of skilled riflemen who spearheaded attacks, were the elite of the Continental Army. Bill White, in his study of the State Garrison Regiment, writes that 85 infantrymen from the State Garrison Regiment volunteered for Porterfield's command. Marshall's Corps of Artillery and two troops of Nelson's Cavalry also became part of Porterfield's command. The total number of men under Porterfield seems to have been around 420.

Because of the British threat on April 7, 1780 Governor Jefferson moved the state government from Williamsburg to Richmond. At the same time, the headquarters of the State Garrison Regiment moved from Williamsburg to Richmond. Only a handful of troops remained in Williamsburg to defend the Powder Magazine and the Public Store.

Porterfield's command left for Charleston March 29, 1780. Charleston fell to the British in May before Porterfield's command arrived. They remained in South Carolina, joining up with General Gates, the hero of the Battle of Saratoga, on August 3.

General Gates planned to surprise the British at Camden, South Carolina, by marching at night. General Cornwallis also undertook a surprise attack. At half-past two, about nine miles outside of town, the morning of August 16, 1780, the advance guard of the Continental Army met the advance guard of the British Army under General Cornwallis. The meeting of two armies in the middle of the night was totally unexpected.

Porterfield's detachment formed part of the advance guard of Gates' army along with Armand's Cavalry and the First Maryland Brigade. When the armies clashed, the Continental cavalry under Armand fled, throwing the First Maryland Brigade into confusion. Porterfield's light infantry restored order, but Porterfield was wounded in the left leg below the knee and captured. After this first encounter, both sides retired. Fighting was renewed the following morning, resulting in a devastating defeat for the Continental Army at the Battle of Camden.

Few members of Porterfield's command made it back to Virginia. As many as one-third of their number fell at Camden. Others were taken prisoners and marched to Charleston and confined in prison ships in the harbor where large numbers died from smallpox, dysentery, and typhus. Colonel Porterfield waited ten days before he received medical treatment. The British took him to Camden by cart where his leg was amputated. Porterfield died five months later on January 10, 1781. He was thirty years old.

A pension application made by Bernard Reynolds on August 7, 1832, reveals the fate of the soldiers of the State Garrison Regiment who escaped from Camden. According to this document, soldiers from Porterfield's detachment reassembled in Hillsboro, North Carolina, and eventually returned to Richmond where they became part of Colonel Charles Dabney's command. They fought at the Battle of Yorktown in October of 1781. The surrender of the British under Cornwallis must have been especially sweet to the survivors of Camden.

In replicating the State Garrison Regiment, the Colonial Williamsburg Fife and Drum Corps honors the soldiers that defended Virginia and fought for liberty. They help us remember the sacrifices that went into the creation of our nation.

The Battle of Yorktown

Fifers and drummers most frequently are remembered in association with the Battle of Yorktown. Continental soldier Ebenezer Denny described his thrill "...seeing and hearing a lone British drummer beat the *Parley* to arrange for the surrender of Lord Cornwallis." Denny like the other military men at Yorktown recognized the beat and knew its meaning.

Legend has it that when the British marched out to surrender, they played the tune *The World Turned Upside Down*. Whether or not the British fifers and drummers played this song is a subject of much scholarly research. As fitting as the title of this tune may have been, there is no record of exactly what music was played. The surrender took place with drums beating and according to one witness, the accompaniment of the fifes. Since each tune only takes minutes to play, the fifers and drummers probably played several tunes although there is no record of the specific music. The important role of the fifes and drums in the armies of the eighteenth century is illustrated by the fact that among the arms turned over by the defeated British army at Yorktown there were 137 fifes and drums.

Another incident related to fifing and drumming occurred at Yorktown. A physician, Dr. Thacher, borrowed twenty-some fifers and drummers whose musical services were not needed. He wanted them to help with the wounded. Thacher recorded the incident because he turned over his medical instruments and bandages to one of the drummers who could not be found when the items were needed. It seems that the drummer had gone off in search of rum. This seems to suggest that fifers and drummers were serving as non-combatants at the Battle of Yorktown.

Does this incident also suggest that the drummer was an older man? Archibald Willard created a painting called *The Spirit of '76* for the Centennial of the American Revolution. Now in the Marblehead Massachusetts Historical Society, it shows two drummers, an aged man and a young boy. A wounded veteran plays the fife. Although this is an imaginary scene, romanticized for the Centennial, fifers and drummers were both young and old. Sometimes, the older men were fife and drum majors who trained the younger musicians. Also, fifers and drummers aged in the ranks and according to their terms of enlistment could not be transferred to regular duties. It seems likely that older men stayed on because they were hard to replace, and fifing and drumming was indispensable to smooth operation of the Continental Army.

Fifers and drummers were present at the beginning of the American struggle for independence and at the end. Throughout the war, their contribution was incalculable. Since that time, the fifer and drummer have become a symbol of American liberty.

Into Modern Times

After the Revolutionary War, fifers and drummers continued as part of the American military. In the last years of the eighteenth century, the Marines employed fifers and drummers on America's men-of-war. Congress ordered the construction of the frigates *United States, Constellation,* and *Constitution* on April 20, 1796. Each ship was to have a Marine detachment. Among the Marines were three fifers and drummers assigned to each ship by a Congressional Act of July 1, 1797. French cruisers and privateers were preying on commercial shipping along the East coast and the government sent the new American ships to eliminate the threat.

The following year, President John Adams established the United States Marine Band consisting of a drum major, a fife major, and thirty-two fifers and drummers. Under the direction of Drum Major William Farr, the band gave concerts in Philadelphia and Washington. They played favorite tunes such as *Yankee Doodle*, *Rural Felicity*, *My Dog and Gun*, and *On the Road to Boston*. Gradually the Marine Band added other instruments and expanded its participation in social events.

President Thomas Jefferson signed a bill in 1802 establishing the United States Military Academy at West Point and fifers and drummers had regular duties there until 1815. In the years that followed, the bugle was increasingly used to sound signals. However, fife and drum corps continued to be an integral part of the military. Fifers and drummers participated in the War of 1812 and in the Mexican War.

The army maintained a School of Practice at Governor's Island, New York, to train boys as field musicians. Augustus Meyers wrote a description of his time at the school in his memoir, *Ten Years in the Ranks, U.S. Army*. Meyers joined the army at age 12 on March 31, 1854. He wanted to become a drummer until he noted the "exceedingly large and heavy drums" the drummers carried. Fifty or more music boys, ranging in age from 12 to 19 lived in crowded barracks, sleeping on bunk beds without pillows. Meyers sums up his living conditions on Governor's Island, "... I had but little liberty, was half starved, and was badly treated in many ways."

Each weekday, the music boys began the day by sounding *Reveille*. At eight they beat *Guard Mount*. Afterwards they policed the grounds and quarters. They had school from nine until eleven o'clock with an hour of private practice before and after lunch. Two hours more of lessons followed. At four, they had instructions in soldiering and company and squad drills. The day ended with *Retreat*. Initially, Meyers received room, board, training, and $8.00 a month pay. Congress raised the pay to $12.00 a month about six months after he enlisted.

The music lessons at the School of Practice emphasized rote learning. The army used two texts in the early days of the school, Ashworth's *Fife Instructor* and Scott's *Instructor for Drum and Fife*. In 1862, the army adopted Bruce and Emmett's *The Drummers and Fifers Guide* as the official text of the school. This book was an improvement over its predecessors in that it not only provided instructions in fife and drum but also spelled out the camp duties of the fifers and drummers. Civil War re-enactors use the text today as a guide to their music and performances. In 1869, a board of officers approved a new text for the school, Strube's *Drum and Fife Instructor*.

At the time of the Civil War the drummers set the cadence for marching and men fired their rifles following drum commands. More importantly, the fifers and drummers regulated the military day with the calls and ceremonies established during the Revolutionary War.

Field musicians during the Civil War were non-combatants. They did not carry firearms. Their only weapon was a small sword on their left hip. Sometimes fifers and drummers were sent to the rear to aid stretcher-bearers and their duties in camp included helping the surgeon.

Lack of standardization at the time of the Civil War resulted in a variety of arrangements for field musicians. In the cavalry and artillery, bugles generally replaced the fifes. In some units bands replaced fifes and drums. Some infantry units had buglers. Others units had bands, fifers and drummers, and buglers. Some units had buglers and bands. Recruiters, according to army regulations of

Library of Congress, Prints and Photograph Division, (LCB8I7-7688)

Civil War Fife and Drum Corps, 10th Veteran Reserve Corps at leisure.

1863, sought boys of age 12 and upwards to be instructed on the "fife, bugle, and drum and other military instruments."

Some of the youngsters serving in the Civil War distinguished themselves. One fourteen-year-old Civil War Union drummer, Orion P. Howe, won the Congressional Medal of Honor for bravery at the Battle of Vicksburg in 1863. Another boy drummer, Johnny Clem, got the nickname "Johnny Shiloh" after his drum was hit at the Battle of Shiloh in 1862.

Not all the boys fighting for the Union were heroic. It came to President Lincoln's attention that a fourteen-year-old drummer was facing execution for desertion. In a letter to Secretary of War Stanton, Lincoln wrote, "Hadn't we better spank this drummer boy and send him home?" Lincoln's sentiments were shared by others who felt that young boys should not be sent off to war. Congress responded in 1864 by banning the enlistment of anyone under sixteen, ending the practice of recruiting young boys as musicians.

Union General Daniel Butterfield introduced *Taps* in July, 1862, while in camp at Harrison's Landing, Virginia. Bugler O. W. Norton worked out the notes that after the war became the official call at the end of each day.

Civil War veterans remembered the music of the fifes and drums long after the war. Veteran Enos B. Vail complains in his memoir in 1915 that "I never read

Posing for photographer Timothy H. O'Sullivan are Civil War fifers and drummers of the 93rd New York Infantry.

any work on the Civil War which mentioned anything about the fife and drum corps." He writes that they constituted "an important part of the army." Another veteran, Delavan Miller, writing in 1905 laments that field music seemed to have gone out of style. "I have heard but one good drum corps since the war, and that was at the G.A.R. gathering at Buffalo a few years ago." Miller reports that at this meeting "the veterans went wild as they heard again the *Reveille* and *Tattoo* ...."

In the years following the Civil War, fifers and drummers – although no longer young boys – did not entirely disappear from the American military. Bugles replaced fifes around 1885 when most of the warfare was on the western frontier. However, it does not seem that the fife was ever totally supplanted. Early motion pictures of the American Expeditionary Force going off to World War I show fifers accompanying them.

An official U.S. military group of fifers and drummers appeared in 1927. The Fessenden Fifes became part of the 4th Marine Regiment stationed in Shanghai. An American, Sterling Fessenden, the chairman of the Shanghai Municipal Corporation and the Civil Commandant of the Shanghai Volunteer Corps, arranged for a number of musical instruments to be given to the 4th Regiment for the formation of a fife and drum corps. The fifers and drummers of the British 1st Battalion, Green Howards, taught the Fessenden Fifes to play music, establishing close ties between the two groups. After the Fessenden Fifes, there was no official fife and drum corps in the American Army until 1960.

Following World War II, a renewal of interest in fifing and drumming developed across the United States and in Europe. Many groups founded fife and drum corps, reenacting various historical periods. Some of these corps began to meet annually for Drum Corps Musters at Deep River, Connecticut.

In 1960, the 3rd US Infantry, known as the Old Guard, established the Old Guard Fife and Drum Corps. Their 11-hole fifes, handmade rope-tension drums, and Continental Army uniforms replicate a fife and drum unit from 1781. They have participated in every Presidential Inaugural parade since 1961. They widely represent the U.S. Army at functions across the United States and abroad.

Interest in fifing and drumming has continued to grow. The celebration of the Bicentennial of the American Revolution and the growth of military-reenactment units contributed to the burgeoning interest. In 1987, the Company of Fifers and Drummers opened a Museum of Fife and Drum at Ivoryton, Connecticut. Today, fife and drum corps exist across the United States and in many other countries.

Fifing and drumming shows no signs of disappearing in America. The tootling of fifes and thundering of drums has become an important reminder of our nation's sometimes-precarious past.

Eighteenth-century Military Music at Colonial Williamsburg

To the visitors at Colonial Williamsburg, the Fife and Drum Corps appears never to change, but to the Corps leaders, members, and alumni it is always changing. Former Musickmaster John C. Moon explains, "Tradition is the key to understanding the Fifes and Drums, and tradition is not written. It is mutable. Tradition is the bricks, discipline the mortar of the Corps."

The Corps is ever changing for a number of reasons. Since its founding in 1958, a steady stream of youngsters has moved through the ranks, each making a contribution. Corps leadership has changed several times, each new staff member building on the foundations of their predecessors. The repertoire has grown, and the Corps' role at Colonial Williamsburg has expanded. Yet in spite of these changes, over the years the devotion to excellence has remained the same.

The idea of creating a fife and drum corps goes back to May 1953. The first mention of the possibility of a corps in the Colonial Williamsburg Archives is a letter from Douglass Adair of the *William and Mary Quarterly* to John Goodbody of Colonial Williamsburg. Adair suggested inviting some fife and drum corps to Colonial Williamsburg and possibly establishing a local corps. Adair thought that fifing and drumming would provide "a dramatic and genuine touch to such celebrations as May 15 and the Fourth of July...." He argued that fifers and drummer were the only inhabitants of North America who "dress in colonial clothes and work in them all the year around" and that the "practitioners of ancient music are genuinely eighteenth-century in their craft."

Bill Geiger, Director of the Craft Shop at Colonial Williamsburg, proposed in July, 1953, the organization of a colonial militia that would include six drummers and two fifers. The militia came into being in 1955, without fifers and drummers. In the early days of the militia, Colonial Williamsburg imported musical groups to support the military unit. Geiger, however, wasn't satisfied with this arrangement. He wanted Colonial Williamsburg to have its own fifers and drummers.

Colonial Williamsburg Vice-president John W. Harbour, Jr., was Geiger's next-door neighbor. In 1958, Harbour had a seventeen-year-old son, Evans, then a 10th-grader at James Blair High School. Evans had just formed a band combo, and Geiger sent him a half-dozen fifes, asking if Evans and his friends would be willing to learn to play them. Because they had no eighteenth-century fife music, John Harbour picked out the notes on the piano to *Yankee Doodle*, the only eighteenth-century music he knew, and Evans wrote them down.

Evans learned the fife along with his friends, J.P. Cottingham, Johnny Ruffin, and Linc Peters. He recruited Allen Lindsey, Talmadge Alphin, and Jim Teal as drummers. Soon the group knew three songs: *Yankee Doodle*, *General Washington's Freestep*, and *The British Grenadiers*.

The fledgling Fife and Drum Corps performed with the militia as part of regular Tuesday and Friday afternoon muster ceremonies. They provided music and trooped the colors during the performances. But still Colonial Williamsburg brought in The Lancraft Fife and Drum Corps from New Haven, Connecticut, for more formal events, like the Prelude to Independence celebrated on May 15.

The organization of the Corps was informal. New members were recruited by word of mouth. The Corps practiced each Saturday and performed twice a week from April through October. Their first home was in the Up and Down Cottage behind Market Square Tavern. Colonial Williamsburg paid Corps members for practices and performances according to a graduated pay scale.

Paying members is one of the reasons for the Corps' success. Over the years, other groups have sought to emulate the Colonial Williamsburg Fifes and Drums.

However, without wages for teenage participants, it is hard for other corps to recruit and keep members, musical commitment taking a second place to part-time jobs.

By 1960, the Corps had grown to 14 members, but they still only knew three songs. Army Sergeant George P. Carroll now entered the scene. He had established the Old Guard Fife and Drum Corps for the Third Infantry, U.S. Army. For reviving this old military tradition, he had received the Army Commendation Medal. Carroll was twenty-seven-years old and had been in the Canadian and American armies for eleven years. He had been selected to form a drum group for Canada's participation in the coronation of Queen Elizabeth II in 1953 and knew over 1,000 songs of the colonial period. He visited Colonial Williamsburg in May, and Carroll offered to conduct summer and fall training sessions for the Corps on his free weekends. At summer's end, the Colonial Williamsburg Fifes and Drums Corps knew thirteen tunes and felt confident enough to enter the South Atlantic Regional Fife and Drum Corps Muster in Arlington, Virginia, where they won second place in the junior division and third place in the senior division.

In June 1961, when his Army enlistment was up, George Carroll came to

George Carroll and the Corps pose in front of the Capitol.

Williamsburg full time as an instructor for the Fifes and Drums. The Corps was still part of the militia, headed by Bill Geiger. Carroll was responsible for research and implementation of colonial military music. It was Carroll who set up an efficient organization for the Corps that had now grown to fifteen members.

Former drum major Jack Reitz remembers, "Carroll instituted the rank system where you passed tunes to move through the ranks. Before that it was a bunch of boys who knew each other getting together for a common purpose." The rank and point systems that Carroll instituted, with some modifications, are still in place. He established classes led by peer instructors and a calendar of events several weeks in advance. He also developed a roll-call system for each activity, a clothing issue and laundry system, and created a repertoire of written music for both the fife and the drum. Under his leadership, Corps membership grew until a waiting list for prospective Corps members became necessary to ensure fairness.

Carroll made the Corps respected at Colonial Williamsburg, in the community, and in musical circles. From its earliest days, the Fife and Drum Corps had many invitations to perform outside Williamsburg. Most of the invitations had to be declined because Corps members had school commitments and their primary role was to support activities at Colonial Williamsburg.

In spite of these limitations, the Corps took a number of trips and participated in various competitions, winning a great number of awards. "We got to the point," Reitz reports, "where we expected to win competitions. If we didn't win first honors, we were disappointed."

Carroll published a small magazine, called *The Drummer's Assistant,* and formed a Band of Musick with himself as Musickmaster to replicate military band music of the eighteenth century. Now, long years after *The Drummer's Assistant* has ceased publication, Fifes and Drums staff still get requests for it. Carroll inaugurated annual musters in 1966 where fife and drum corps from several states came each fall to Colonial Williamsburg for fifing and drumming competitions.

In 1967 Herb Watson, a clarinet and a recorder player and member of the Band of Musick, began working part time for Colonial Williamsburg. He became a full-time employee in 1968. With the title of Music Assistant, Watson helped Carroll run the Fife and Drum Crops. Watson, gray-haired now, still plays eighteenth-century music at Colonial Williamsburg. He recalls, "A lot of times there was pandemonium trying to get the programs out before the public." He describes one particularly stressful morning. "We were in Cameron Hall at Eastern State

Hospital and then we moved to the Old Courthouse next to the Lodge. The first Saturday we were in the new location, we had an 8:30 a.m. performance called The Beating of the Drums. We got there at 7:45 and Bill Gieger, the boss, arrived when we were having roll call. I was making assignments for the kids, trying to talk to Gieger, and time was at a premium. There is a lot of sweat, toil, and worry, putting on a program."

Nineteen seventy-one was a year of transition and testing. The Corps suffered a tremendous loss with the untimely death of Militia Director Bill Geiger in December 1970. "Bill Geiger was an energetic person who was dedicated to the eighteenth century and a big supporter of military music," Watson recalls. Gieger's enthusiastic support had been essential in the founding and the development of the Fifes and Drums. His death was followed six months later in June, 1971, by the resignation of George Carroll. Carroll left to accept a position at Disney World. By this time, there were 26 fifers and drummers in the Corps, and it was housed in the Old Courthouse. The repertoire had grown to 63 tunes.

While searching for a new Musickmaster for the Corps, Watson took over the administration of the Corps and eighteen-year-old Corps member, Bill White, was in charge of the music. White was sergeant major under George Carroll and even before he left, White had assumed a leadership position. The self-governing aspects of the Corps established by Carroll were so effective that the group went through this change of leadership with no significant problems. They performed as usual and took what by now had become their annual trip, traveling to Sturbridge Village and Mystic Seaport.

Carroll had contributed much to the Corps. Under his direction, they had grown from a small, informal group of friends to an elite, award-winning unit that played, not only for Colonial Williamsburg, but also at places like West Point, Valley Forge, the Canadian National Exhibition, and the World's Fair. Carroll had fostered pride and esprit de corps that did not disappear when he left Williamsburg. Watson recalls, "It was a thrill to work with the kids, George, and later with John Moon. Carroll was a very strong personality so naturally not everyone agreed with him. George didn't always do the politically correct thing."

Corps members liked Carroll. "He was a dynamic leader," recalls Reitz. The boys were "in awe of the man's musical ability. Carroll picked up his drumsticks and beat on everything." He taught Corps members a lot, exposing them to different types of music. He put the Corps on the road to excellence. His expectations were high, and the Corps responded. Recalling the many competitions the

Corps won, Reitz recalls, "We did it for George, but for ourselves, too."

Carroll's shoes would be difficult to fill, but the second Musickmaster, John C. Moon, who came to Colonial Williamsburg in January 1972, was up to the task. He had extensive experience as a British military musician. He had been a boy soldier in the Scots Guards and at age 23 became the youngest drum major in the Guards. While serving as drum major and drummer to the Royal Household, Moon supervised the training of new arrivals and boy soldiers. He toured widely with the Scots Guards band and was five times in charge of the Massed Bands at the Edinburgh International Festival Tattoo.

John Moon directing five fifers and a bagpiper during Christmas activities in 1975.

Moon's leadership created a lasting legacy for the Corps. Now retired, Moon still maintains an erect, military bearing and speaks directly, inspiring confidence. He is clearly a man with high personal standards. He believes that "good enough is just not good enough," and this injunction continues to inspire the Corps. He maintains that discipline should be constant and cover all aspects of Corps activities and that managed progression leads to steady improvement and strength at all levels. Moon emphasizes that responsibility and trust should be constant, like discipline. Although most of his life had been involved with music, he has a clear sense of priorities. "The building of character and good citizenship within the group," he says "is more important than the apparent end product, in this case, music."

During the first week at Colonial Williamsburg, Moon established his first directive: "All activities will start on time." Since then, the punctuality of the Fifes and Drums has set the standard for other performances and departments at Colonial Williamsburg.

The Fifes and Drums had been established to support the militia. Under Moon's direction the Corps began to have its own calendar of events. The new Musickmaster began a whole series of innovative programs including *Reveille*, *Retreat*, and a *Drum Head* church service. It was Moon who taught the Corps slow marching for ceremonial pieces, and he began to use Corps members as street musicians to entertain visitors more casually. He established a library for Corps records, music, and associated music literature. Like Carroll before him, Moon's main job, besides guiding the Corps along, was to research and arrange eighteen-century music.

One of the improvements that Moon brought to the Corps was the establishment of the Junior Corps as a training ground for the Senior Corps. This enabled musicians to have an apprenticeship of two to four years before joining the Senior Corps. Not long after this, the Junior Corps began to have its own schedule of performances, and seeing the little boys march quickly became a popular program at Colonial Williamsburg. By 1974, there were 78 members in the Corps, and the repertoire was then at 280 tunes.

Esprit de corps grew in the Moon years. The interaction of local boys with the stern, but fair Moon gave rise to a series of stories. Moon tells of one day when the whole Corps showed up in their shirts, regimental uniform vests and jackets, and their boxer shorts. Unfazed by this, Moon responded, "You are all out of uniform. Minus five points." Lance Pedigo, current Corps Supervisor, relates that one of his worst memories as a Corps member came when he set a new drum sideways on a stool and it rolled off, breaking the rim. He had to tell Mr. Moon about it. He was pretty upset, Pedigo explains, and Moon did *not* tell him that it was "all right."

Moon's management of the Corps was widely admired in the community. His injunction that: "Discipline is another word for love" impressed Corps members and their parents. Parents urged the school superintendents of Williamsburg-James City County and York County, the school systems that serve Williamsburg, to meet with Moon in January 1975 to discuss Corps disciplinary methods. Although discipline in local public schools could not emulate the Fifes and Drums program, there was a strong consensus in the community that Moon was doing something right.

By the late 1970s, Colonial Williamsburg President Longsworth felt that the Fifes and Drums should be the signature group for the historic village. Throughout the years the Corps had been in existence, they had occupied makeshift buildings for lessons, practices, and staff offices. After the Up and Down Cottage, the Corps moved to the Prentis Store Building for a while, then to the basement of the Old Eastern State Building. By the 1970s, they were in the Old Courthouse Building. It was time for the Corps to have a fitting facility. After several years of planning, a new Fifes and Drums Building opened in March 1981.

During the Bicentennial of the American Revolution, a special celebration was held in October 1981 to commemorate the victory over the British at Yorktown, the last major battle of the Revolutionary War. As part of this celebration, the Corps marched from Market Square in Williamsburg to Yorktown. They retraced the steps of colonial soldiers two hundred years before. The Fifes and Drums were accompanied by the militia unit from Colonial Williamsburg, Minute Men from Concord, Massachusetts, five regiments of the Southern Battalion of the Yorktown Bicentennial Brigade, two covered supply wagons, a scout on horseback, and approximately 30 camp followers.

Courtesy of Colonial Williamsburg

Dylon Pritchett leading the Corps out of Williamsburg for the 15-mile march from Williamsburg to Yorktown in 1981.

The march began at 10 a.m. on October 15 in mid-40 degree temperatures and ended seven and a half hours later at the Yorktown battlefield. The Corps, led by drum major Dylan Pritchett, played for the whole fifteen-mile march down the Colonial Parkway. The marchers took an hour break for lunch at one-thirty, and three brief rest breaks. As they

Tired drummers rest, sitting on a curb near the Williamsburg Regional Library.

marched, the day warmed and sunlight filtered through the trees that line the Colonial Parkway. The handmade colonial shoes were stiff and unforgiving, and some Corps members developed blisters. The base drummers carrying the 16-pound drums had the hardest jobs. Yet, they all pluckily marched on, taking pride in not complaining.

At 5:15 the marchers drew in sight of the crowds gathered at the Bicentennial Celebration. The Fifes and Drums were cheered when they proudly marched onto the battlefield playing *Point of War* followed by *Three Taps, Three Cheers.*

The 15-mile march to Yorktown helped to dramatize some of the realities of Revolutionary War fighting. In the eighteenth century, after a long day marching, the soldiers had to set up camp and prepare meals before their night's rest. Fifers and drummers, as military timekeepers, had to perform duty calls and *Tattoo* before their day's work was finished. The re-creation of the march from Williamsburg to Yorktown was one of the inspiring moments of the Bicentennial Celebration, exemplifying the sacrifices that made possible American independence.

The march to Yorktown was indicative of the ways Moon found to promote the Corps. Throughout the Moon years, the number of performances of the Corps at Colonial Williamsburg continued to grow. According to Moon's records, in 1982 Senior Corps hours spent working totaled 15,642 with an average of 474 hours per member spent in Corps activities. The Corps still received many invitations to appear in the United States and Canada. They usually took at least one major trip each year. In spite of the energy crisis of the 1970s, the Corps performed at West Point, Gettysburg, Valley Forge, the Highland Games in Delaware, Philadelphia, New York City, and the Canadian National Exhibition in Toronto.

May is always a difficult time of year for the Fife and Drums Corps. With final exams in school looming just ahead in June and Colonial Williamsburg gearing up for the summer season, fifers and drummers find themselves especially busy. The most challenging May for the Corps came in 1983 when Colonial Williamsburg hosted the G7 International Economic Summit on Memorial Day weekend.

During the Economic Summit, leaders of seven industrialized nations met for a series of discussions on economics and political issues. They all arrived and departed separately: President Ronald Reagan representing the United States, President Francois Mitterand from France, Prime Minister Margaret Thatcher from England, Prime Minister Pierre Trudeau from Canada, Chancellor Helmut Kohl from Germany, Prime Minister Yasuhiro Nakasone of Japan, and Prime Minister Armintore Fanfani from Italy. John Moon recalls, "The Corps played for seven arrivals and seven departures, and many times in between." So much playing can be hard on any group, and especially on school-age kids. "Some of the arrivals and departures were at two o'clock in the morning. It was a crowning moment."

In June 1983, Musickmaster Moon, now in charge of the Company of Colonial Performers, turned over direction of Corps activities to Bill White. Before this time, the leadership of the Corps had been brought in from outside. White became the first former Corps member to head the Fifes and Drums. Since White had grown up with the Corps, it is understandable that he would emphasize for others what had worked so effectively in developing his own leadership skills.

After only four years as Corps Supervisor, White switched positions with Moon in 1987. Moon resumed the leadership of the Corps until his retirement in 1991. White continues at Colonial Williamsburg as Executive Producer and Director for Educational Program Development. His two sons, Charles and William, have both served in the Corps. The family is proud of more than three decades with the Fifes and Drums.

Courtesy of Viky Pedigo

As Musickmasters, Carroll and Moon had handled instructions in both fifes and drums. In 1991, Corps leadership passed to two people. With Moon's strong emphasis on the importance of tradition, it was no accident that in seeking new leadership for the Corps, Moon and White looked to former Corps members, Tim Sutphin and Lance Pedigo. They both knew and understood the history and traditions of the Corps.

Tim Sutphin's expertise is fifing while Lance

Lance Pedigo proudly wears his Senior Corps uniform.

Lance Pedigo leads the Corps through the Historic District of Colonial Williamsburg.

Pedigo's proficiency is drumming. Sutphin had been a Corps member from 1975 to 1983 and became a field music instructor for the fife in 1988. He took over as Manager of the Corps when Moon retired. Pedigo had begun drum lessons under George Carroll and joined the Corps under John Moon in 1972 at the age of nine and had been sergeant major for three years before graduating from high school in 1982. After college he worked as a professional musician until taking the position of Corps Supervisor of the Fifes and Drums.

A considerable part of Sutphin's and Pedigo's work is continuing to research and arrange eighteen-century music. But their positions involve much, much more. They are role models, leaders, teachers, and disciplinarians. Sutphin, like Moon before him, sees his main role as teaching youngsters responsibility.

Under the direction of Sutphin and Pedigo, the high standards of performance and excellence continue. In addition to their other duties, the Corps still represents Colonial Williamsburg on trips and in the community. According to Bill White, the latest musical recording on both compact disk and tape, made in 1996, is the best in a series of recorded music. Part of the reason is because it was digitally mastered for the best accuracy, but mostly the reason is that the fifers and drummers are excellent musicians, and the music calls for the fullest display of skill. Several Corps members were so proud of this recording that they included copies of it with their college applications.

The Corps is still evolving. In 1997 and 1998, Colonial Williamsburg moved in the direction of performances in smaller enclaves. The Corps is an integral part of these new programs. According to Lance Pedigo, "this is a more authentic approach to presenting the role of the fifes and drums in the eighteenth century." Some older programs, like *Reveille*, will be no longer performed.

Perhaps the greatest single evolutionary step in the Corps' history is the admission of girls. When the Fifes and Drums Building was built in 1981, a woman's locker room was installed with the idea that eventually the Corps would recruit girls. Over the years, a number of girls had asked to join the Corps. The Colonial Williamsburg Foundation resisted these on the grounds of historical inaccuracy. Yet, the Colonial Williamsburg Fife and Drum Corps was the only corps in the country that didn't admit girls. Finally, in April 1998, the Colonial Williamsburg Foundation announced they were advertising for a female instructor. This was a preliminary step to recruiting girls.

Opinions pro and con appeared in local papers. In spite of any reservations they might have had, the fifers and drummers supported the decision of the Colonial Williamsburg Foundation. "I still remember the day they told us about it. It was a rainy Tuesday," Haislip says. "I thought *The World Turned Upside Down* would have been an appropriate tune."

In November 1998, Amy Edmondson Miller joined the Corps as the new field music instructor. With a Ph.D. in flute performance from Florida State University, Miller had a strong background in early music. She is a petite, slender young woman with honey-colored hair and bright brown eyes. She speaks softly as she explains, "I started out as if I was going through the program in the Junior Corps, passing tunes and learning to march. My transition into the Corps was to go through the same training as a fifer. By the time the first class of girls arrived in the fall of 1999, I had passed up to sergeant."

Miller reports that "only one or two girls have decided the Corps wasn't for them." The dropout rate for the girls is about the same as that for the boys, Miller says. Sometimes girls come to talk with her, but boys do too. Besides interacting with the other Corps members, Miller has a lot of administrative duties, and she occasionally arranges music for performance by the fifes and drums.

During her second year with the Corps, Miller taught a class with a Senior Corps member. In teach-

Amy Edmondson Miller discusses her time with the Corps.

Author's photograph

ing the class before she was fully proficient with the repertoire herself, she gained the experience of peer teaching that is so much a part of the tradition of the Corps. "It didn't take me long to learn that mastering my job as field music instructor was a long-term project." Although she still feels that there are parts of her job that she has yet to master, she believes that she belongs to the group. "To be an authority figure, you have to be considered one of the fold. Part of that was working into things slowly. Every year, I feel more and more a part of the program."

Miller marches with the Corps and occasionally a visitor asks: "Are you a girl?" Miller isn't upset by such queries. "I'm out there to look like a guy," she says. "If they can still tell the difference that's fine, but if they can't that's okay, too. It means the illusion works."

The addition of girls to the Corps was a big move, but it seems to have gone smoothly. As the Corps grows and develops, much remains the same. Corps members are part of a small, unique group. Whatever changes come, the Corps' high standards and great expectations remain constant.

That Special Something

Many ingredients contribute to making the Colonial Williamsburg Fifes and Drums so special. Three things stand out: the marches, the music, and the years of practice. For Corps members the marching and the music are inseparable. On occasion they play when not marching, but the music is most compelling when set to the motion of marching feet.

Everyone loves a parade. Several times a week the Fifes and Drums march. Sometimes it is the Junior Corps; other times it is the Senior Corps. When the Fifes and Drums are playing, marching is contagious. Bystanders catch the spirit and step off with the Corps. It is hard to explain exactly what is going on. What are the spectators thinking about when they follow the Corps? Are they thinking at all? Or are they, for a few minutes, going back in time to march to the

The Senior Corps dodges raindrops.

Author's photograph

Corps members are confident that they are the best at what they do.

defense of a new nation whose rising star is more vision than reality?

William H. McNeill, in his book, *Keeping Together in Time: Dance and Drill in Human History,* suggests that rhythmic movement produces an emotional feeling that "the group is one." Part of the special bond shared by the members of the Fife and Drum Corps may be more than being united in a common pursuit from the ages of ten to eighteen. Rather the special cohesion of the group may arise from marching together. Miller explains that "On a march everyone is focused on the same thing. You feel your place in a formation on an axis. You have to feel yourself as a spoke in a wheel." People who march together have to rely on each other. The Corps is the sum of its part, and it's only as good as the lowest corporal.

McNeill also suggests a relationship between rhythmic motion and trances. Fifers and drummers report that when they march they are in another world. Are they simply tuning out tourists and distractions? Or are they tuning into the music as they march? John Moon agrees that marching can induce a trance-like state. This practical, no-nonsense, former soldier says, "It can take you up." Pedigo admits being "lifted up" when marching, but he is not sure it is spiritual. Haislip comments, "I loved how the music could take you in, swallow you up and turn you into part of a much larger being, a part of a vast body, eliminating your individuality, or perhaps rescuing you from it for a short time."

It is difficult to access the effects of the music on Corps members. In asking Corps members what they learn from their experience with the Fifes and Drums, a standard reply is "music." The shared music is a strong bond not only among members of the Colonial Williamsburg Fifes and Drums, but among other fifers and drummers. When a visiting corps comes to Colonial Williamsburg, the music creates a community of interest.

The Junior Corps marching in the snow.

What music is played, and how well it is played, is important to Corps members. They are always learning new pieces. For every rank, there are new tunes to learn and the repertoire is always growing. New music keeps the performances fresh and helps prevent Corps members from growing bored with constant repetition of the same songs.

It is challenging to be always learning new music, and Senior Corps members like to play hard music. If they learn something new and difficult and then play it well, they are pleased with their performance. If a tune doesn't go well during a performance, then the whole group will be in a bad mood.

Former Musickmaster Moon maintains that Corps members never fully learn their instrument until they become teachers themselves. One of the strengths of having the older Corps members teach the younger fifers and drummers is that both groups become better musicians.

Once tunes have been studied, practiced, committed to memory, and taught, they become a part of the fifer or drummer. Therefore, when Corps members or former Corps members get together, it is often to play music. Sometimes at performances, someone in the audience will request a particular tune. When the tune requested is *Black Bear* or *The Quick Step Medley*, the fifers and drummers guess that a former Corps member is in the audience, longing to hear again an old favorite. By the time a boy or girl has been in the Corps for seven or eight years and as a Senior Corps member knows two to three hundred tunes by heart, is it any wonder that these pieces sometimes need to be played, if not formally with the Corps, then informally among friends?

To get a sense of the extent of the music the fifers and drummers know, spend time with summer street performers. It reveals both the quantity and quality of music these young musicians have committed to memory. If a fifer or drummer spends all day playing tunes, the music must leave a lasting impression on the performers.

Practice, then, is one of the secrets of the Corps' musicianship. Beginning modestly in the recruit year, the time commitment grows with each year a fifer or drummer stays in the Corps. By the time the fifer or drummer leaves the Corps, he or she has had seven or eight years of practices, lessons, and performances. Years of practice produce a high level of proficiency.

Fifers and drummers realize that the Corps is special. They have a clear sense that they are an elite group. They believe that they are the best at what they do. This feeling of elitism is underscored by the enthusiastic reception that the Corps gets at Colonial Williamsburg and when they represent Colonial Williamsburg in other capacities. The boys and girls usually do not know music when they join the Corps. Mastery comes gradually. It is little wonder that after years of lessons, practices, and performances, Corps members are confident that they are the best at what they do.

A Community of Fifers and Drummers

A shared tradition creates great loyalties. Strong ties are tested when someone dies. On several occasions, Corps members have played at the funerals of other Corps members. Bill White felt that one of the hardest things he has ever had to do was to play for fellow Corps member Tommy Williams' funeral when he drowned in Queen's Lake in 1976. A picture of Williams hangs in the Fifes and Drums Building and each year fifers and drummers elect one of their number to be the recipient of an award, in Williams's honor. Years later, Lance Pedigo asked Anthony Jackson, twice a winner of the award, to play *Chester* at Tommy Williams' mother's funeral. "It was the hardest performance I ever did," Jackson recalls. "People sobbed in the background." Yet Jackson considers this performance among his three most memorable in the Corps. In 1981, two Corps drummers, alumni Dale Bowen, and Richard Morrison Carter were killed in separate automobile accidents on the same day. Other Corps members were devastated and volunteered to play Bowen's graveside service. The death of former Corps mem-

Author's photographs

At the Corps reunions, the fifers and drummers in uniform march alongside Corps alumni.

Author's photographs

At the annual Williamsburg Christmas parade, Corps alumni march proudly behind the Fife and Drum Corps'
banner.

ber Rick Blood on September 11, 2001, made the memorial service at Burton Parish Church one year later especially poignant.

Loyalties and friendships go hand in hand. At some point Corps members start becoming friends, instead of merely members of the same group. This result is that they often get together socially. The occasion may be informal like going to a movie or more formal like playing for one another's weddings. Over the years, Corps members have formed sports teams. Whether the sport is an informal game of softball, volleyball, ultimate frisbee, or league soccer, the fifers and drummers enjoy extending the team work of the Corps to the playing field.

Even when Corps members aren't friends, they have tremendous loyalty to each other. Tim Sutphin explains that in the eyes of the Corps members "the lowest Fife and Drum Corps member is still above everyone else." It is like a family. Members may not always agree. Yet there is family solidarity. Jack Reitz described an incident when the Corps withdrew to protect their drums when it began to rain. A drum and bugle corps taunted them and "both groups brandished drumsticks at each other." It never came to a battle, but Corps members were ready to defend each other. "There is something about a group of people pulling together for a common cause," Reitz said. "You get a real oneness."

Once Corps members graduate this doesn't mean necessarily that they are through with the Corps. A few fifers and drummers informally get together at the Fifes and Drums Building. Dylan Pritchett, for example, joins Lance Pedigo and Tim Sutphin at the Fifes and Drums Building to play music. Pritchett is still an excellent fifer. Some members used the fife or drum to relax from the complications of their adult lives. Other former fifers and drummers have sons or daughters in the Corps. John Ruffin has founded his own corps in California.

A group of former fifers and drummers living in the Williamsburg area formed a group called Williamsburg Field Musick. They play at various functions throughout the area and strive to incorporate into their music, the high standards of performance and professionalism learned in the years with the Colonial Williamsburg Fifes and Drums.

Even after many years, loyalties to the Corps remain firm. Alumni of the Corps have been known by various names: "The Bastard Corps," "The Orphan Corps," or "The Ghost Corps. " These sad names suggest a sense of separation from the real Corps. There is separation, but still connectedness. "It is kind of strange to this day, to think that I am out of the Corps. Perhaps it is more a temporary leave of absence," Haislip says.

Former Corps members have been eager participants in the two reunions held in recent years. One hundred-twenty former Corps members showed up from across the country in 1993 for the thirty-fifth anniversary of the Corps' founding. Inspired by the music of the current Corps, the alumni picked up instruments and marched along with the youngsters up Duke of Gloucester Street led by Dylan Pritchett, drum majoring with a broom. "A goodly number of the old group from the 60s come to the reunions," Watson says. "It shows the loyalty of the group and that the experience must have meant a lot to them."

Over 90 former Corps members gathered for the fortieth anniversary in 1998. Again, a Corps of veterans marched along with the current fifers and drummers, pausing at Market Square to play informally in groups. Afterwards everyone marched back to the Fifes and Drums Building. Old friendships were renewed and new friendships formed.

Starting in 2000, alumni began performing in the annual City of Williamsburg Christmas Parade. They wear Santa hats and follow a banner held by current fifers and drummers, recognizing them still as affiliated with the Colonial Williamsburg Fifes and Drums.

The loyalties to the Corps are easy to understand. The average person has few, if any, opportunities in life to be part of something greater than himself or herself. However successful the individual may be in his or her career, it is not the same as being part of an elite group with the highest standards of performance and self-discipline.

These strong loyalties are part of the Corps tradition. The boys and girls change, but the Corps stays the same. Corps members come with commitment day in and day out. They put in years of practicing. They perform in all weather from blazing sunshine to blowing snow and sleet. The days pass, the years pass, their time passes. But when they are dismissed for the last time, they go away with the knowledge that they were part of something bigger than themselves. Watson says what all fifers and drummers know. "I love seeing the Corps march in straight ranks, hearing the reverberations of the drums off the buildings in Market Square, and knowing that I had a little bit to do with it."

Sources

Manuscripts

Moon, John C. <u>A Compendium for the Fifes and Drums of Colonial Williamsburg</u>. Unpublished Manuscript. John D. Rockefeller, Jr. Library, Williamsburg, Virginia, Fall, 1994.

Moon, John C. <u>A Proposal to Establish and Maintain A Military Regimental Band.</u> Colonial Williamsburg Foundation Library Research Report Series. Manuscript Booklet, "Music of the Fifes and Drums," Appendix F. John D. Rockefeller, Jr. Library, Williamsburg, Virginia, 1984.

White, William E. <u>The Virginia State Garrison Regiment</u>, 1778-1782. Colonial Williamsburg Foundation Library Research Report Series-321. John D. Rockefeller Library, Jr. Library, Williamsburg, Virginia, 1990.

Williamsburg, Virginia. Colonial Williamsburg Foundation Archives. Colonial Military Unit Records. General Correspondence, 1952-1977; Press Releases; Meetings–Presentation Division.

Williamsburg, Virginia. Fifes and Drums Library: Correspondence, Michael Sweeney to Tim Sutphin, Lance Pedigo, and Corps members, August 16, 1998.

Interviews

Jackson, Anthony L. Telephone interviews . 20 August 2002; 12 September 2002.

Miller, Amy Edmondson. Personal Interview. 19 September 2002.

Moon, John C. Personal Interview. 15 September 1997.

Pedigo, Lance. Personal Interview. 22 October 1998.

Prittchett, Dylan. Personal Interview. 18 September 1998.

Reitz, Jack. Personal Interview. September 1997.

Sutphin, Timothy. Personal Interview. 14 October 1997, 7 October 1998; telephone interview. 9 October 2002.

Watson, Herb. Telephone Interview. 24 September 2002; 25 September 2002.

White, William E. Personal Interview. 13 August 1997.

Woodard, Kaitlyn. Personal Interview. 15 September 2002.

Books

Baum, Howard S. <u>Organizational Membership</u>. Albany: State of New York, 1990.

Camus, Raoul F. <u>Military Music of the American Revolution</u>. The university of North Carolina Press: Chapel Hill, 1976.

Cellini, Benvenuto. <u>Autobiography</u>. Baltimore: Penguin, 1966.

Farmer, Henry George. <u>The Rise and Development of Military Music</u>. London: W. Reeves, 1912.

Fitzpatrick, John C. <u>The Spirit of the Revolution</u>. Port Washington, NY: Kennikat Press, 1970.

Howard, John Tasker. <u>Our American Music</u>. New York: Crowell, 1965.

Lewis, Andrew. <u>Orderly Book</u>. Richmond: Privately Printed, 1860.

Lord, Francis and Wise, Arthur. <u>Bands and Drummer Boys</u>. New York: Da Capo Press, 1979.

McIlwaine, H.R., ed. <u>Official Letters of the Governors of Virginia. Vol. II. The Letters of Thomas Jefferson</u>. Richmond: Virginia State Library, 1928.

McNeill, William H. <u>Keeping Together in Time: Dance and Drill in Human History</u>. Cambridge, MA: Harvard University Press, 1995.

Meyers, Augustus. <u>Ten Years in the Ranks, U.S. Army</u>. New York: Arno Press, 1979.

Miller, Delavan S. <u>Drum Taps in Dixie</u>. Watertown, N.Y.: Minuteman Press, 1990.

Olson, Kenneth E. <u>Music and Musket: Band and Bandsmen of the American Civil War</u>. Contributions to the Study of Music and Dance, Number 1. Westport, CT: Greenwood Press, 1981.

Parker, William D. <u>A Concise History of the United States Marine Corps, 1775-1969</u>. Washington: Historical Division, U.S. Marine Corps, 1970.

Peterson, Harold K. <u>The Book of the Continental Soldier</u>. Harrisburg, PA: Stockpole Books, 1968.

Rabelais, Francois. <u>Gargantua & Pantagruel</u>. Baltimore: Penguin, 1955.

Roberts, Michael. "The Military Revolution" in Orest Ranum, ed. <u>Searching for Modern Times</u>. New York: Dodd, Mead and Company, 1969.

United States. Army Inspector General Friedrich von Steuben. <u>Regulations for the Order and Discipline of the Troops of the United States: Part I</u>. Philadelphia: Styner and Cist, 1779.

United States. Continental Congress. <u>Journals of the Continental Congress, 1774-1789</u>. Washington, DC: Government Printing Office, 1904-1937.

White, William C. <u>A History of Military Music in America</u>. Westport, CT: Greenwood Press, 1975.

Wilbur, C. Keith. <u>Picture Book of the Continental Soldier</u>. Harrisburg, PA: Stockpole Books, 1969.

Periodicals

Coblentz, David H. "Virginia's Charles R. Porterfield," <u>Manuscripts</u>. 18 (Summer, 1965): 29-30.

Goldman, Michael, "Marching in Time," <u>Boys' Life</u>. 88 (July, 1998): 28-30.

Montgomery, Dennis, "If Ponies Rode Men and Grass Ate the Cows," <u>Colonial Williamsburg Journal</u>. 21 (October/November, 1999): 33-39.

Moon, John C., "The Fifes and Drums of Williamsburg," <u>Colonial Williamsburg Journal</u>. 2 (Spring 1980): 4-7.

Olmert, Michael, "Military Music in the 18th Century," <u>Colonial Williamsburg Journal</u>. 11 (Summer, 1989): 7-12.

Tolbert, Bill, "Lure of Fife and Drum Corps Endures Time," <u>Williamsburg Magazine</u>. (September, 1993.)

Theobald, Mary Miley, "Cooperman Fife and Drum: A Family Enterprise." <u>Colonial Williamsburg Journal</u>. 11(Summer, 1989): 339-42.

Waddell, J.A. "Diary of a Prisoner of War at Quebec." <u>The Virginia Magazine of History and Biography</u>. 9(October, 1901): 144-152.

Newspapers

Aron, Paul, "Economic Summit," <u>The Virginia Gazette</u>, 19 November 1997.

Bruno, Susan, "New Fife and Drum Building Designed to be Energy Efficient," <u>Newport News Daily Press</u>, 6 February 1981.

Bruno, Susan, "Trek Ends in Yorktown for Soldiers," <u>Newport News Daily Press</u>, 16 October 81.

Erickson, Mark, St. John, "Beat of a Different Drummer," <u>Newport News Daily Press</u>, 3 July 1994.

Hatton, Nigel D. "Like Father, Like Sons: Family has Corps Tradition," <u>Newport News Daily Press</u>, 14 August 1996.

"Losing 2 Friends In A Day Heavy Burden for Youths," <u>Newport News Daily Press</u>, 13 May 1981.

McLaughlin, Bill, "First in Fifes," <u>Newport News Daily Press</u>, 31 January 1990.

Straszheim, Deborah, "Girls to Play Fifes, Drums at CW," <u>Newport News Daily Press</u>, 24 June 1998.

Straszheim, Deborah. "Opinions Vary over Girls in Fife Corps," <u>Newport News Daily Press</u>, 25 June 1998.

Internet Sources

"US Bands in History" http://bands.army.mil/history/firstarmyregulation.asp

Cifaldi, Susan. "The Drummer Who Waited On Washington." 2001: The Company of Fifers & Drummers. http://moylan.info/bks/achmet/

Keene, R. R. "After 200 Years, the Marine Band Plays On," <u>Leatherneck</u>, The Magazine of the Marines. http://www.mca-marines.org/Leatherneck/bandpomp.htm

Leach, Joseph K. "The Birth of the US Army – Concord." http://www.grunts.net/wars/18thcentury/birth/concord.html

Lester, Charles S. "Selected Speeches from the Celebration at Schuylerville, October 17, 1877." <u>The Centennial Celebrations of the State of New York</u>. Albany: Weed, Parsons, and Company, 1897. "Burgoyne's Surrender" http://www.fortklock.com/Burgoyne.htm

Olson, Ed. " The History of Fifing and Drumming."
http://companyoffifeanddrum.org/tcfdamer. html

Reynolds, Bernard. Revolutionary War Pension Application. <u>Law Order Book</u>, 9,
August 7, 1832. p. 383. http://www.rootsweb.com/~varussel/other/
reynolds.html

Santelli, James S. "A Brief History of the 4th Marines." Marine Corps Historical
Reference Pamphlet. http://www.au.af.mil/au/awc/awcgate/usmchist/
4thMar.txt

Selig, Robert A. "The Revolution's Black Soldiers."
http://www.americanrevolution.org/blk.html

Webern, Robert W. "Fifes and Drums." http://www.worldmilitarybands.com/
drumsfif.html